YALE HISTORICAL PUBLICATIONS

LEONARD WOODS LABAREE · EDITOR

MANUSCRIPTS AND EDITED TEXTS

XVI

PUBLISHED UNDER THE DIRECTION OF
THE DEPARTMENT OF HISTORY
FROM THE INCOME OF
THE FREDERICK JOHN KINGSBURY
MEMORIAL FUND

THE

Parliamentary Diary

OF

Sir Edward Dering

1670–1673

EDITED BY

Basil Duke Henning

Instructor in History
Fellow of Saybrook College in Yale University

New Haven: Yale University Press
London: Humphrey Milford: Oxford University Press
1940

Copyright, 1940, by Yale University Press
Printed in the United States of America

TO MY MOTHER

Preface

THE Diary is contained in Add. MS. 22,467 in the British Museum. It covers one hundred and nine folios in a bound volume and is entirely in Sir Edward Dering's hand. Many passages are underlined, or a line is drawn beside them in the margin. I do not know who did this, but the ink is of a different color from that used in the entries, and I surmise that this underlining was done a good while after the Diary was written. Consequently, these underlinings are indicated in footnotes rather than italics.

In this edition, I have modernized spelling and punctuation throughout. When a member is recorded as speaking in the House, his name is printed in small capital letters; if he spoke in committee, lower-case letters are used. As far as possible, I have, in paragraphing, attempted to separate action from speech.

Every editor of a parliamentary diary must be grateful for the model furnished by Wallace Notestein and Hartley Simpson. I have particular reason to be grateful to them for many constructive suggestions. For much sound advice I am indebted to William H. Dunham. Richard P. Arms and Douglas Heck have been most helpful with clerical assistance. A Sterling Fellowship made it possible for me to complete this edition; for that I wish to thank the Graduate School of Yale University.

B. D. H.

New Haven, Connecticut,
February, 1940.

Introduction

UNTIL historians are able to describe in detail the working of the Restoration parliaments, the tangle of Restoration politics cannot be undone. Diaries of M.P.'s describing proceedings provide the best of materials for the study of parliament; unfortunately the period which produced so many private memoirs has so far been comparatively barren in parliamentary diaries. Sir Edward Dering's is the third Restoration diary to be printed which is completely devoted to parliamentary business.[1] Dering was no Pepys or Reresby; he never mentions personal matters (except to note his occasional fits of the ague) and it is only between the lines of his diary that his personality emerges. He appears as a man who was modest and moderate, who wanted to get things done, and above all, as a man who loved and respected order.

This last quality is best displayed by Dering's great interest in procedure. He was a stickler for correct methods—"it is necessary to observe the old order of the House better than now we do"—and he was fascinated by the details of parliamentary business. Consequently, there is scarcely an entry which does not contain a reference to procedure. He writes of proper and improper motions; of the way questions should be worded; of the confusion resulting from the Lords' amendments to the Commons' bills; of procedural difficulties in committees. And these matters are of importance to the general historian as well as to the parliamentary specialist, for Dering makes it plain how both parties used parliamentary order to further their own policies and thwart those of their opponents.

1. *Debates of the House of Commons from the Year 1667 to the Year 1694*, collected by Anchitell Grey, was published in 1769. *The Diary of John Milward* (*1666–1668*), edited by Caroline Robbins, was published in 1938.

Dering was much more interested in procedure than Anchitell Grey, and this is one reason why the chronological correspondence between the accounts of the two men does not detract from the value of Dering's Diary. In addition, Dering reports fifty-one days which are omitted in Grey's *Debates;* on twenty-four other days the two reporters record entirely different debates; and there is scarcely an entry in the Diary which does not provide a valuable cross-bearing on the *Debates,* or furnish additional knowledge of parliamentary activity. The form used by Dering, like that employed by John Milward, is much clearer than Grey's. By reporting each speech separately, Grey gives to his account a vividness which is lacking in Dering, but what Grey gains in color, he loses in clarity. Dering apparently took notes during sittings, and very shortly thereafter worked them up into narrative accounts of each day's proceedings. The words of the speaker he did not attempt to record but his meaning, and since he regarded each debate as a whole, his narrative is easy to follow. While Dering was particularly careful in outlining his own arguments and those of his own side, he did not neglect those of his opponents; the Diary is personal in the sense that Dering sets down his own opinions of the matters under debate, but it is not overly biased.

The diarist, the second baronet, was a member of a Kentish family whose residence in the county is said to date from Saxon times. The family estates at Surrenden, Kent, can be traced to the fifteenth century, and at the beginning of the seventeenth century the family was prominent in local and national affairs.[2] The diarist's father was that Sir Edward Dering who, out of zeal for the Protestant religion and a fondness for primitive episcopacy, proposed the first reading of the Root and Branch Bill. But he soon entered the royalist and Anglican ranks, and at the outbreak of the first civil war, raised a cavalry regiment for the King. Sir Edward

2. Burke, *Complete Peerage, Baronetage, and Knightage* (1937), p. 879; Wotton, *Baronetage,* I, 263; Hasted, *History of Kent,* I, 136.

was not happy in military service; by 1643 he had resigned his commission, and he was one of the first to make his peace with the parliament.[3] He took the covenant on February 7, 1643–4, and on July 27 it was recommended that his fine be £1000, his estate being valued at £800 per year. He had died, however, on June 22, and his widow, his third wife, was discharged of the necessity of payment.[4]

At this time his heir, the second Sir Edward Dering, was eighteen years old. His mother, Anne Ashburnham, had been old Sir Edward's second wife and had been dead since 1628.[5] A daughter, Elizabeth, was also born of this marriage. A third marriage had given Edward two half sisters and two half brothers, one of these, unhappily, being named Edward also.[6] The diarist, Edward, was first educated at London, then at Surrenden, and entered Sidney Sussex College in 1640. The next year he was admitted to the Middle Temple, but in October, 1642, he returned to Cambridge, this time to Emmanuel College, and he took his degree early in 1643. In April of the next year, he may have entered the University of Leyden, but if so, it is likely that his residence abroad was short.[7] That he returned to England at his father's death is probable, and he lived at least part of the time in the Middle

---

3. *The Dictionary of National Biography.*

4. *Calendar of the Proceedings of the Committee for Compounding,* pp. 831–2.

5. G. E. Cokayne, *Complete Baronetage,* II, 6.

6. Burke, *Peerage,* p. 879. This Edward Dering, "of London, merchant," was knighted January 6, 1679–80 (Shaw, *The Knights of England,* II, 254). He was probably the Edward Dering who had commercial dealings with the navy in the sixties (*Cal. S. P. Domestic, 1660–1,* p. 212; *1661–2,* p. 426), and who was, by 1683, governor of the Merchant Adventurers, or, as they were then called, the Hamburg Company (E. Brinkman, "England and the Hanse under Charles II," *English Historical Review,* XXIII, 708). The epitaph of the diarist, inscribed in the church at Pluckley long after his death, states that he was governor of the company, but this is almost certainly a mistake (*Archaelogia Cantiana,* X, 340). There is no other evidence to show that he had any connection with the Hamburg trade, whereas his half brother certainly did (*Cal. S. P. Domestic, 1670,* p. 708).

7. Venn, *Alumni Cantabrigienses,* II, 36; C. H. Hopwood, ed., *Middle Temple Records,* II, 917. Sir Edward certainly wished to go abroad. In a

Temple where he had a chamber which he relinquished in November, 1647.[8] His marriage in the following year to Mary Harvey, the daughter of Daniel Harvey, a rich city merchant, is further evidence of a London residence.[9]

During the next fourteen years, Sir Edward seems to have divided his time between Surrenden and London. His circumstances were fairly comfortable, for his account book shows that from 1648 to 1652 his household expenses alone ran from four to five hundred pounds a year.[10] Most of his income was derived from his estates, but he may also have been interested in the Turkey trade.[11] During this period his life was private;

letter dated February 29 (but no year is given) he asks his father to get him a pass from the Speaker to go into France (Add. MS. 26,785, f. 68). In a letter printed in the 1771 edition of Wotton's *Baronetage*, IV, 439, it is stated that at the time of the first baronet's death his heir was "a minor, and beyond sea."

8. Hopwood, ed., *Middle Temple Records*, II, 956.

9. The wedding took place at St. Bartholomew's the Less on April 5, 1648 (G. E. Cokayne, *Baronetage*, II, 6). This was perhaps Lady Dering's second venture. Sir Robert Twysden wrote in his notebook that she "was indeed contracted if not married to one William Hanke, her cousin and her father's servant, one that had been his apprentice but was now free. He, in a morning going through Colmans Street with her, got her very young into the church, and with a ring did marry her about 1645, and caused it to be registered in the book of marriages of the church. She was in this to be excused because he assured her he had her father's assent, which he never had; but her speaking very softly at the time so as it could not be deposed she did assent unto it; and her that very day returning him his ring, and disclaiming it, and never suffering him to come near her, and her youth capable of being deceived; with the good friends her father made prevailed so far that after a legal hearing in the Ecclesiastical Courts (for they were not then quite put down) she was by sentence cleared; and being after to be married to Sir Edward Dering, 1646 or 1647, her friends and she told him all the facts, and showed him her sentence for being free under the seal of the court; and they have lived very lovingly ever since. She a good wife and a means of advancing the family" (Add. MS. 34,164 f. 95). Hasted, who says he got the story from "a late respectable clergyman of Kent" (but long afterwards), asserts that Hanke bedded with her twelve months, and that the marriage was discovered on the occasion of her marrying Sir Edward (Hasted, *Kent*, VII, 469).

10. Add. MS. 22,466.

11. The Earl of Winchilsea in the notes for a letter to Sir Heneage Finch, November 12, 1660, stated that if he obtained the Lisbon Embassy he would resign his Turkey employment to Sir Edward Dering (*Historical Manuscripts Commission, Reports, Finch*, I, 86).

his name does not appear on the commissions of the peace, and it was only just before the Restoration that he took an active part in public affairs. Under the act of March 12, 1659–60, he was named a commissioner of the militia for Kent, an appointment which indicates an enmity to the Commonwealth.[12] Sir Edward served as deputy lieutenant under the Earl of Winchilsea, who declared "that he is not only a very sober and wise man, but very well affected towards our King and church."[13] Dering soon had had an opportunity to show his good affection in a larger field; he was chosen to represent Kent in the Convention Parliament.[14]

Sir Edward was an active member of this short parliament. He was named for twenty-two committees; this shows that he took part in the reconstruction of the national life. He had a hand in framing the bills which abolished feudal dues, fixed a revenue for the King, settled the militia, and began the settlement of the church.[15]

There is no evidence that Sir Edward sought re-election in 1661. Perhaps he had been given notice of other employment in store for him; at any rate, in July, 1662, he was appointed one of six commissioners for executing the act of settlement in Ireland, a position which he held until the commission was dissolved in 1669.[16] In 1667 he was sworn of the privy council of Ireland, and in the same year he was given a more material reward with the reversion of the office of auditor-general of that kingdom.[17] Ormonde, the lord lieutenant, regarded him as "an able and loyal servant" and wrote to Arlington that he was of "excellent parts and proportionate in-

12. C. N. Firth and R. S. Rait, *Acts and Ordinances of the Interregnum,* II, 1433.

13. Stowe MS. 744, ff. 45, 48.

14. Cobbett, *Parliamentary History,* IV, 4.

15. *The Journals of the House of Commons,* VIII, 11, 107, 181, 187. Dering was also on the committee of elections and privileges.

16. *Cal. S. P. Ireland, 1660–2,* p. 577.

17. *Ibid., 1666–9,* pp. 347, 483. Dering never actually held this office; on November 9, 1678, its reversion was granted to his son Charles (*Cal. S. P. Domestic, 1678,* p. 513).

dustry";[18] in short, a gentleman who would be valuable in the King's service. Sir Edward did not have long to wait before entering that service. Scarcely six months after his return to England, he was appointed one of the commissioners of the privy seal,[19] and in November, 1670, he was returned for East Retford, Nottinghamshire, an election which was fully as much an evidence of court favor as had been his appointments to offices.[20]

Dering's parliamentary life, which continued through all the parliaments of Charles II, was an exceedingly active one.[21] He spoke often (Grey records seventy of his speeches), and of the more than two hundred committees for which he was named, forty-one dealt with matters of political importance.[22] In the period covered by his diary, he was constant in his attendance, and it is likely that in the later sessions he was as regular.

Sir Edward belonged to the court party. He so regarded himself,[23] and his name is found on the lists drawn up for the ministers and on those published by opponents of the court.[24]

18. *Cal. S. P. Ireland, 1666–9*, pp. 331, 337.

19. Haydn, *The Book of Dignities*, p. 240. The privy seal was put in commission during Lord Robarte's absence in Ireland.

20. *Official Returns*, I, 526. Five years before Sir Edward had tried to get a seat in Kent or the Cinque Ports. His son-in-law, Sir Robert Southwell, one of the clerks of the council, corresponded with Arlington about the business, but Arlington was unable to find Dering a place (*Cal. S. P. Domestic, 1665–6*, p. 121; Stowe MS. 744, f. 105). East Retford was under the control of the Duke of Newcastle, and according to Henry Savile, who wanted the burgess-ship himself, it was "the court recommendation" which decided Newcastle in Dering's favor (W. D. Cooper, ed., *Savile Correspondence*, p. 25). Sir Robert Southwell accompanied Dering to East Retford, and wrote that the election was unanimous (*Cal. S. P. Domestic, 1670*, p. 522).

21. Sir Edward was returned for Hythe to the next three parliaments (*Official Returns*, I, 539, 545, 551).

22. Sir Edward was also ten times on committees of elections, and was chairman of the committee of the whole House during the important subsidy debates in February and March, 1677–8 (*Commons Journal*, IX, 434–50).

23. See below, p. 57.

24. E. S. de Beer, "Members of the Court Party in the House of Commons, 1670–1678," *Bulletin of the Institute of Historical Research*, XI, 7.

By the latter he was regarded as a placeman, an accurate opinion, no doubt, for his connection with the government was surely a profitable one. His post as commissioner of the privy seal netted him altogether £2290,[25] and in 1673 he was granted a pension of £400, which he received until 1676.[26] In December, 1675, he had been appointed a commissioner of customs for tonnage and poundage at an annual salary of £1200,[27] and when his commission was withdrawn in the spring of 1679, he was made one of the lord commissioners of the Treasury at £1600 a year.[28]

Thus Sir Edward had from the government more than fifteen thousand pounds,[29] but it was paid as much to the administrator as to the M.P. He was, essentially, a moderate man. Often in the House he sought compromise between factions, and while he "would have the King treated with all reverence,"[30] he was by no means always subservient to the royal will. For Dering belonged to the anti-French and anti-Catholic front. He was thus a follower of Danby, but when that minister fell under suspicion, Dering served on the committee which drew up the articles of impeachment against him.[31] In the hysteria of the Popish Plot, Dering seems to have been swept along with the majority of Englishmen. He served on most of the important anti-Popish committees formed at the beginning of the excitement, yet, ironically enough, he was himself labeled a Papist in a pamphlet of Dr. Tonge;[32] an

---

25. He was allowed £5 per day (*Calendar of Treasury Books*, III, 293).
26. *Calendar of Treasury Books*, IV, 415, *et passim;* V, 232.
27. *Ibid.*, IV, 869.
28. *Ibid.*, VI, 4, 265, 728. Sir Edward held this office until his death. He was also one of the commissioners appointed to inquire into abuses in the mint (1677–8), and a commissioner for recusants' lands in 1675 (*ibid.*, IV, 788; V, 751, 986). He was also, of course, many times a justice of the peace. (P. R. O., Petty Bag Office, C. 193:12, 13; Patent Rolls, 13 Car. II, part 31, 14 Car. II, part 20, 17 Car. II, part 3; C. 66:2986, 3022, 3074.)
29. There is no record of his salary as an Irish commissioner, but the six commissioners were allowed £20 per week for their table, and £1 5s. each for lodgings (*Cal. S. P. Ireland, 1666–9*, p. 142).
30. Grey, *Debates*, IV, 26.   31. *Commons Journal*, IX, 560.
32. *The Popish and Damnable Plot against our Religion and Liberties*

allegation voted "false, scandalous, and libellous" by the Commons.[33] Sir Edward was not named for the committees which drew up the Exclusion Bill; he opposed it at its first proposal, but he voted for it when it came up again. Even at this time, however, he hoped for harmony between King and Commons; he never believed in pressing Charles too far.[34]

And he retained the confidence of his King. In 1680, when the commissions of the peace were purged, he remained on the lists for Kent and Middlesex (though his son Edward was left out) and in May of that year, he lent the exchequer £1800.[35] It is difficult to tell what Dering would have done had he lived through the Revolution. His sons were strongly Whiggish (Daniel was suspected of complicity in the Rye House Plot)[36] and Sir Edward was a zealous Protestant. But he was also a trusted and trustworthy servant of the Crown, and had James retained him in office, his oath of allegiance might have weighed heavily in the balance. Death, however, discharged the necessity of so painful a choice. On June 24, 1684, he died in his house in London.

He was a long time in dying. An account of his last days has been preserved in a letter from his son Charles to Sir John Perceval, and it gives, I think, some of the flavor of Dering's personality. "On Tuesday, the 17th, in the morning," runs the letter, "my father got up to go to the Treasury, but finding himself indisposed, was persuaded to go to bed again, but in the afternoon, finding himself a little better, he rose

Fairly Laid Open and Discover'd in the Breviats of Threescore and Four Letters and Papers of Intelligence. In this pamphlet (p. 23) it was stated that Sir Edward had corresponded with Rome. This accusation was, of course, absurd; Tonge declared that Sir Edward's name had been printed by mistake (Stowe MS. 746, f. 40).

33. *Commons Journal,* IX, 654.
34. Grey, *Debates,* VIII, 277; *Historical Manuscripts Commission, Reports,* XII, App. IX, p. 111.
35. *Ibid.,* XI, 181, 184; *Calendar of Treasury Books,* VI, 554.
36. His house was searched for arms (*Cal. S. P. Domestic, 1683,* p. 117). He was also one of those named in the Meal Tub Plot (Grey, *Debates,* VIII, 2).

and went to the Treasury, but came home ill, complaining he was very cold, went to bed, and the next morning found himself feverish, but thought it nothing; but in the afternoon, his fever growing higher, he sent for Dr. Betts, who he had a good opinion of, both by reason he had just before done very well with me in my fever, and because he had been with him in a fever he had thirteen years ago, when everybody thought he would have died. When the doctor came he ordered him something to take—the Jesuits' powder it was—and assured us he would do very well, and that there was no danger at all. Thus he continued very hot and restless, without any intermissions, but once, until Saturday morning, and then he complained of a sore throat, and could hardly swallow. The doctor apprehending it might prove a thrush, and knowing how fatal they had been of late when they came with fevers, desired my mother to have another doctor, and proposed Dr. Barwick, who was sent for, who when he came concluded it was a thrush. All this while poor father, though he was very uneasy, was not at all apprehensive of danger, nor indeed was any of us, the doctors were so positive he would do well. On Sunday morning my brother Dering came to town and whether it were for joy to see him or that he was a little more at ease I cannot tell, but he was very cheerful, and consequently we in no fears. Thus he continued till Monday night, and then about twelve at night he sent for my brother to come to him, and then told him he should die, and therefore desired him to see that he had beer enough, which, he said, the nurses denied him; 'for,' says he 'since I must die I will die playing the good fellow in small beer'; he said, also, that he should die like my Lord Chancellor, for though some people called his the gout in the stomach, it was no otherwise than a sore throat, and says he, these are special physicians that cannot cure that. The next morning, notwithstanding all this, when the doctors came, they were so confident that they assured my mother that he would do well, and ordered him some blisters, which at eleven o'clock the night before they had thought not necessary. In the afternoon, we finding him to grow worse, notwithstanding the doctors, my brother desired my father that he might call Dr. Lower, who my mother had been against. My father said, with all his heart. When he came he told us (but not my mother) that he could not live, for having inquired after his manner of illness, and what had been done to him, he positively said that all had been done three days too late, and though they had let him blood twice, yet it was three days too late. Notwithstanding all this, when Dr. Lower was gone Dr. Betts assured my mother that he would do well, and at seven o'clock at night my mother came into us with all the joy that could be, that she had great hopes my father was mending, upon which my brother going in to see, felt his pulse the most disorderly that could be, and finding him crept just to the outside of the bed, and gathered up all of a heap, asked him how he did; he said he was crept into a narrow corner of the world, and by and by they would shove him out. After this he got up (for he still kept his strength) and sat in his chair and then bid my mother fetch his will and read it, and if there was anything in it she would have altered to tell him, so that will was fetched and read, and he asked if she were satisfied, and then he gave us his blessing, and bid us fear God and be faithful to the King. And now was the first time my mother despaired of him, for he began to have 'convulsions' in his hands and his lower jaw, so that we were forced to get her upstairs into another chamber. After this he walked with little or no help from his chair to his bed, and said he would lie down never to rise again. My brother asked him if there was anything else that he would have done; he said that he had nothing more to do but die; and so in a quarter of an hour he went away without the least groan or sign to the great amazement of us all."[37]

37. *Historical Manuscripts Commission, Reports, Egmont,* II, 139.

THE PARLIAMENTARY DIARY OF
SIR EDWARD DERING
1670–1673

Tuesday November 15, 1670[1]

THE Speaker, according to order, left the chair at ten of the clock and the house resolved into a grand committee to consider of the King's supply.

Resolved to lay an imposition upon all wrought silks imported from beyond sea.

Resolved, an imposition upon thrown silk (that is, spun silk) that is brought in spun.

This received some opposition because the weaving of it after it is spun is done here in England and the weaving is ten times as considerable a manufacture as the throwing it, but it passed in the affirmative.

[Wednesday] November 16[2]

THE House was held very long in a report of privilege claimed by the Lord Newburgh, a member of the House of Commons, against the Duke of Richmond, his son-in-law, a member of the House of Lords. The case is thus: [*blank*].

Resolved at the grand committee for supply to lay an imposition upon all woollen stuffs and hair stuffs, or stuffs mixed with hair, wool, or silk, that are imported wrought.

Thursday November 17[3]

THE House turned into a grand committee.

1. In the *Debates,* Grey confines himself to the discussion of Lord Newburgh's affair.
2. Grey has three pages on the Newburgh case but does not mention supply.
3. Omitted in Grey.

Resolved to charge all imported sugars; viz., 1 farthing on sugars from our own plantations; 2*d.* per pound musionado sugars from other countries, as Brazil, Portugal, etc.; some higher duty upon loaf sugar imported.

Much was said against this, as that which would wholly break our trade with Portugal from which we have no other returns for our says and serges and perpetuanas which are carried thither in good quantity, but it passed.[4]

[Friday November] 18[5]

RESOLVED in the grand committee to lay 5*s.* per cent upon all currants imported, and 2*s.* per cent upon Malaga raisins, and 3*s.* upon raisins of the sun, and 12*d.* upon figs and prunes.

Much was objected against this as what would lessen our trade with Spain—the most beneficial trade we have; but it passed.

Resolved, an imposition upon nutmegs, cinnamon, mace and cloves imported.

It was said that this would signify nothing, for now the customs was only due; yet nothing is paid, for it is always stolen, and much more will be so if the duty be doubled.

It was allowed by all that spoke on it that it would signify nothing at all to the King to be paid at the customs house, only the first buyer; these things being always brought in privately in little creeks or even in the sailors' trunks and in their pockets.

Then Colonel Birch offered if they would lay the duty by way of licenses upon all the retailers, it would be worth to the King 80,000*l.* per annum.

It was presently observed that one way would bring in nothing, the other way a vast revenue, and that we should choose what is best for the King.

---

4. See V. M. Shillington and A. B. Wallis Chapman, *The Commercial Relations of England and Portugal*, pp. 205–221.
5. Grey confines himself to the discussion on currants.

But Birch would not make out his proposal in any manner of degree; and Mr. Joliffe, a merchant, said that all the spices brought into England were not worth 12,000 per annum; and* Mr. Garraway spoke sharply against that way of licensing retailers as what would destroy all trade, calling it arbitrary and tyrannical. Nor did anybody reprove him for it, it being free for any member to speak his sense of what is proposed before the committee for the House have declared their opinion in it.

So it passed at last, for an additional duty to be paid by the first buyer.

[Saturday November] 19[6]

THE debate in the committee was concerning copper plates imported.

The question was put whether half a crown should be put upon the hundredweight, and carried in the negative.

Then it was the question whether any duty should be laid upon them, and Mr. Seymour, who was chairman of the committee, putting it in these words—"All that would have no imposition laid upon copper plates say aye, all that are of a contrary mind say no"—it confounded the committee so, that they knew not how to give their votes, for they who were for the affirmative were to give a negative vote, and who were for the negative, an affirmative, for the question ought not to have been put so, but plainly, thus: All that would have an additional duty imposed on copper plates say aye, all that are of contrary mind say no.

But in this disorder the question passed and was carried in by the affirmative noes.

Then they put the question for how much should be imposed upon the hundred and put it for 5s. and in the same

* *And Mr. Garraway . . . declared their opinion in it* underscored in MS.
6. Omitted in Grey.

disorder the committee, being not recovered out of it, carried it for 5*s.* per cent.

Which I note because I take it to* be irregular and unparliamentary to put the greater sum after the lesser had been put and carried in the negative, for all that had voted that half a crown should not be imposed were concluded from voting of 5*s.;* and this may one day be of ill use, for I believe it has not been known done before and it is necessary to observe the old order of the House better than now we do.

Monday [November] 21[7]

THE House sat very late; viz., till five after noon and yet continued very full.

The business before us was introduced by a motion to consider of some scandalous libel dispensed by women in the hall and given to the members at the House door; from there it was moved to consider the further suppressing of all the sect of Quakers. But soon after it appeared all this was but to introduce into our consideration the suit at law now depending in the exchequer court between Jekyll and Hayes, citizens of London, and Sir Samuel Sterling, last year lord mayor of London, and Sir John Robinson, and Sir Andrew King, and the rest of the deputy lieutenants of London, who had in May 1670 committed to prison the said Hayes and Jekyll for refusing to give security for their good behavior, they looking upon them as suspected and dangerous persons, and that being the time the act against conventicles[8] was to begin to be put in execution.

It was moved by some that Sir Samuel Sterling might come in to the Bar of the House and there inform them what he knew concerning that matter.

It was moved by others that we were not concerned in it,

* *To be irregular . . . in the negative* underscored in MS.
7. Grey's account of this debate is fuller than Dering's.
8. 22 Car. II, c. 1.

it being no way touching upon our privilege but a personal thing between themselves, and the law was open. We* could not hinder any person grieved from bringing his action, nor could we so act but that the judges would proceed according to law.

But it being the sense of the House to call him in, as SIR THOMAS MERES† said it always was and always will be, because there is news in the case, which we are always glad to hear, it was ordered Sir Samuel Sterling should be called in. Then it was desired that Jekyll and Hayes should be called in at the same time that they might hear their accusations. But it was thought more proper to hear Sir Samuel first alone and then to call them in, for possibly it might not concern them at all, possibly there would not be weight enough in it to deserve to trouble them. It might be also some of them might be concerned which we might consider of before it went out of our own walls.

So Sir Samuel Sterling being first called in gave us a relation that about a fortnight before the act was to take place Hayes came to him and asked him what he intended to do in execution of the said act. He answered to put it in execution according to his duty. Hayes dissuading him, the lord mayor answered that there was a penalty if he did not of an 100*l*. Hayes said it was but one hundred pound if he never acted at all and he and his friends would secure him three hundred if he would not meddle in it. My Lord Mayor said he was of opinion that it was 100*l*. for every offense *toties quoties*. Hayes said if it were, he and his friends would secure him from that penalty. My Lord Mayor then rebuking him for offering to bribe a magistrate from doing his duty, Hayes replied: "Well, my Lord, consider what you do, for you have an estate and must look one day to answer for it." Much other discourse he repeated but these were the words the weight was laid upon. Against Jekyll he said he had very little to say.

* *We could not hinder . . . according to law* underscored in MS.
† SIR THOMAS MERES . . . *news in the case* underscored in MS.

But hereupon he called the lieutenants together, and they upon debate thought fit to desire Jekyll and Hayes to give security for their good behavior, which they refusing they committed them to prison from where they were delivered by their* *habeas corpus,* and now brought their actions for false imprisonment.

My Lord Mayor being gone out, the clerks of the House took in writing the sum of what he said, and calling him in again, read it to him, and he owning it to be true in substance, then Hayes was called in, who utterly denied any such words or any private communication whatsoever between him and the lord mayor about such matters, and offered witnesses of what passed between them.

But since it was not probable that such words should be spoke before witnesses, and that my Lord Mayor had acted very ingeniously and very successfully for securing the peace of the city at a time of great danger, there being one Sunday, as he affirmed, at least 12,000 people assembled at the several meeting places contrary to the act; and the King being at that time at Dover with Madame his sister; and the King having, as was said, given instructions to the lieutenants at London to secure such persons as were dangerous; and it being only desired of them to give security for their good behavior, which was most easy for them to do, and which indeed is no more than justices of peace in their several counties may require from persons of ill fame; and it being thought absolutely necessary to support the credit of those deputy lieutenants who had acted vigorously and faithfully for the King's service, it was thought fit by some vote of the House to countenance and justify what had been done in this case.

It was moved to have an act to indemnify the lord mayor and the rest of the deputy lieutenants for what they had done; but that was thought laid some little blemish upon them as though they had committed some fault.

* *Their habeas corpus . . . for false imprisonment* underscored in MS.

It was moved to order the attorney general to put in an information against Hayes and let it go in so; but that was not thought enough.

It was moved to give the lord mayor and the deputy lieutenants the thanks of the House for what they had done; but that was thought unusual and improper.

At last about three after noon or more the House came to a vote: that what the lieutenants had done in committing of Hayes was for his Majesty's service and for preservation of the peace of the kingdom and they did* approve of their proceeding therein.

Then Jekyll was called in, who made a long speech at the Bar, and at last the House resolved that [which] was done in his commitment was also for the service of the King and peace of the kingdom. But the words of approbation and allowance they did purposely leave out, there appearing indeed much less reason for any suspicion upon him than upon Hayes.

Then they ordered also that Mr. Attorney General should put in an information against Hayes in the king's bench. And a committee to inspect the law against conventicles and concerning the militia, and present the defects.

Tuesday [November] 22⁹

THE committee entered upon the business of iron. The Sussex gentlemen were very earnest for to have 40s. per ton imposed upon all iron imported, but the sense of the committee not to have; only 10s. per hundred which was voted and no more.

1. Because iron is a commodity we cannot want, not having enough to supply ourselves.

2. Because it is the consumption of timber trees though it seems an advantage to coppice woods.

---

* *Did approve of their proceeding therein* underscored in MS.

9. Grey reports a debate on the augmentation of vicarages, and one on new buildings.

3. Because there is not 40 makers of iron in all England but every man uses it.

4. Because the tax which will come to the King by this duty is not the 40th part of what will be paid by the subject since every horseshoe, etc., will be made iron.

5. Because it is a tax upon all the farmers especially for their plough, iron, and cart wheels.

6. Because the Swede is the best confederate we have; because it will cost 20*l.* more in building a ship of 100*l.* and so proportionally for a greater bulk; our iron if we had enough being not tough enough for that use.

[Wednesday November] 23¹⁰

SIR JOHN PRETTYMAN was at the Bar there heard by his counsel. He had been suspended the House by an accusation brought against him that he had refused to take or commit one Hume upon a complaint of a rape against him though he had the opportunity of doing it and was often himself in his company. But he producing some witnesses to prove his endeavors to seize him at the ports, the witnesses against him proving nothing at all of their allegation, he was discharged of that imputation and restored to his place in the House.

SIR JOHN BIRKENHEAD spoke of forgery and other ill things he was guilty of, but nothing being proved as to the matter then before the House, the House would not hear him.

Then they resolved into a grand committee, and voted ten shillings per barrel upon every barrel of rum imported; Sir Nicholas Cary, who moved it, saying that rum is bought of the merchants at 50*l.* per barrel, every barrel holding 50 gallons, and is sold at 60 per quart which is 5 pound to the barrel.

Then Colonel Titus moved for a tax to be laid upon all periwigs, and much was said for and against it, and likely to

10. Grey omits this debate on supply.

come to a serious debate, though it was by some raised into a discourse no ways becoming the gravity of that House.

Till Col. Sandys stood up and said he had something of more importance to acquaint us with and desired that [the] Speaker might take the chair, which he did.

And then COL. SANDYS presented the House with an order made that day by which Jekyll had moved for a *venire* in the exchequer to try the case between him and Sir Andrew King concerning the cause of his imprisonment by the lieutenants of London which the House had voted upon Monday last after so long debate to have been done for the service of his Majesty and preservation of the peace of the kingdom. This was aggravated very highly as the greatest affront imaginable, that contrary to the declared sense of the House in the very face of the votes of the House any man should dare to call that an injury and a wrong which the House had declared to be done for the safety of the King and kingdom; that if we* were justly sensible of the privilege of any particular member, we ought much more to be so of the honor of the whole House, and therefore it was moved that Mr. Jekyll and his attorney and counsel might be sent for in custody and answer their contempt at the Bar.

It was said of the other side that Mr. Jekyll had no notice at all of the order of this House and therefore could not be in contempt; that if he had notice thereof yet the very words of that order do not impose any prohibition from his bringing or continuing his action, nor could reasonably be understood so, the House having *de industria* and expressly left out of their vote concerning Jekyll the words of their allowance and approbation of his commitment.

And it was said by MR. HAMDEN that in truth there was† not so much as an order in the case, but a bare vote which ordered nothing at all, and that this could not properly be

* *We were justly . . . of the whole House* underscored in MS.
† *Was not so much . . . at all without doors* underscored in MS.

taken notice of at all without doors, much less be construed a prohibition for any man to proceed in a due course of law when he think himself wrong.

Upon the whole debate resolved that Mr. Jekyll and his attorney and Mr. Burton, his counsel, be sent for in custody.

Memo: For the attorney, SIR WINSTON CHURCHILL averred that he had notice of the order of the House of Commons in this case. But no such thing said of the counsel.

Then after this in the grand committee for the King's supply the motion was made and seconded, and the debate grew very warm about raising a year's rent upon all buildings erected near or in London or Westminster upon new foundations since the act of indemnity. It was said to the contrary:

1. That this was not just, for they had broke no law.

2. That this was not a tax so much as a fine or mulct which should not be laid where there is no crime.

3. That most of them which had built had built by the King's leave under letters patent.

4. That building was no nuisance, but rather an advantage to the health of the inhabitants.

5. That the population of the kingdom was increased and their safety too by the greatness of this city, able to make head against all foreigners.

6. That by the statute of 39 Eliz. all buildings in market towns were allowable.[11]

The committee divided upon it, and the ayes were 77, and the noes were 78. I were in the negative for the reasons above.

Thursday [November] 24[12]

AFTER some private bills read and debated, it was moved to call in Mr. Jekyll with his attorney and counsel. It was con-

11. 39 Eliz., c. 1.
12. Grey's and Dering's reports are similar.

sidered first what the Speaker should say to them and it was thought fit only to read the vote of the House to them. They being called in, MR. SPEAKER put Mr. Jekyll in mind of the large and fair hearing he and his witnesses had had on Monday before the House, and what resolution the House had taken therein, which that he might not pretend ignorance of, he was commanded by the House to acquaint him. Whereupon the clerk read the votes to them, and THE SPEAKER advising them thereafter to behave themselves like discreet men, they were commanded to withdraw.

Memo: They did not kneel at the Bar, as most do that are brought thither in custody, and the Speaker being put in mind thereof, after they were withdrawn, by MR. SEYMOUR, he answered that where prisoners were sent for only *ad prependendum,* they did not use to kneel (which is a distinction I think will not hold).

But they being withdrawn, it was moved by SIR JOB CHARLETON that now they would be more insolent than ever, for they had been called in and only desired to be discreet thereafter [which] was in effect to bid them use their own discretion how far they would respect the orders of the House, so that we were now in worse case than if we had never meddled with it.

And much was said pro and con, many thinking the Speaker had said too much, many too little, and SIR WILLIAM COVENTRY* made a long speech showing us the inconveniences we were running upon by prohibiting any man in his action at law, and that undoubtedly the Lords, who have much greater pretensions to judicature and to inspecting what is done in inferior courts than we can have, will take notice, and either quarrel with us for meddling with a power of judicature which we have not, or at least proceed to exercise the like power by interposing their authority in all cases in Westminster Hall; and how can we offer to defend the right

* SIR WILLIAM COVENTRY underscored in MS.

of the Commons in such case if we ourselves have first used such a power?

By this most people began to see we had gone far enough, and wished for a good opportunity of coming fairly off from it; and SIR ROBERT HOWARD averring that to his knowledge Jekyll was willing to withdraw his action and would not have proceeded so far if he had known the sense of this House to be against it; this was looked upon as a good occasion, for what a member* says of his own knowledge is never doubted to be true; and most being willing to close with it, and others arguing that it should be put off and they continue in custody till they did petition, the question was put for their discharge; and the House being divided the ayes that were for it were 105 and the noes were (I take it) 79, and they were discharged accordingly. I were for the affirmative.

Friday [November] 25[13]

MOST of the morning spent upon a bill of Sir Phillip Howard's, to grant him by act of parliament the benefit of his new invention for the dressing of ships by a thin mixture of lead and other things which will save the ships from the worms and save the necessity of sheathing them.

Memo: He has already a patent from the King for 14 years according to the statute,[14] and has also a patent or grant for the sole use of it for 25 years from the States of Holland.

1. The objection to this: that many others did already use lead to that purpose.

2. That Sir Edward Hungerford, now of the House, has already the same invention and desires he may be a partner therein.

3. That 14 years is enough and a sufficient compensation for his invention.

---

* *Member says . . . to be true* underscored in MS.
13. Omitted in Grey.   14. 21 Jac. I, c. 3.

4. That at least it is not reasonable that England should be longer barred the public use of this invention than Holland is, and they have granted it for 25 years and this bill demands it in England for 31 years.

5. That it does not appear what the invention is, and that it may be said if anyone hereafter does find out any other new invention relating to the better dressing of ships, that this is Sir Phillip Howard's invention.

To the 1st is answered that some do use lead and so they may do still, the bill restraining no man from what is already in use, but only from making use of these materials so prepared as by Sir Phillip Howard is invented; to the 2nd, that Sir Edward Hungerford had never made any use of his invention, if he have it, never owned it nor desired any advantage by it, whereas Sir Phillip Howard has proceeded very far in it both with the King here and with the States abroad, and that however Sir Edward Hungerford has no right to graft his own advantage upon Sir Phillip Howard's bill which only is before us; to the 3rd, that the invention, being very useful and advantageous to the whole nation in their shipping, ought to have greater encouragement than every ordinary mechanical conceit; and that the parliament had passed an act to the Marquis of Worcester for 90 years for the sole use of his water-commanding engine;[15] to the 5th, that Sir Phillip Howard shall be bound within six weeks after the bill passed to publish his receipt and invention in writing and enter the same in court of record, and that this might be done and ordered in the bill itself; and upon the 4th objection the bill was recommitted and not put to the question for engrossing.

Then the House turned into a grand committee to proceed in the King's supply, and voted an imposition of ten shillings upon every French beaver, and less rate upon felts and demi-castors.

15. 15 Car. II, Private acts no. 15.

Then Sir John Knight moved that there might be a license to transport wool with a good duty of custom thereupon; and that this would bring the King 300,000*l.* per annum and yet no more wool exported than now is by stealth. But this proposition was looked upon by many as very dangerous and totally destructive to our English manufacture, and all carried it was not fit to be made in the committee; he might move it in the House if he thought fit.

Then Sir Robert Howard proposed an imposition upon all paper used in going to law, and in bills and answers in chancery, and upon certioraries, records, grants, and patents, and the like, which was put off to further consideration, but seemed agreeable to the sense of the House.

Then the Speaker taking the chair, it was ordered Mr. Seymour should report tomorrow morning what the committee had agreed upon, and that every day at ten we would leave all business whatsoever and proceed upon the King's supply.

Saturday [November] 26[16]

MR. SEYMOUR, according to order, reported to the House what had been agreed at the committee; and the report being read in the House and the particulars put in order, the House agreed to several of them.

The greatest debate was upon home-made salt; and the question being put whether salt made in Ireland should be charged equally with salt made in England, it was carried in the affirmative, and after that they charged upon salt both made in England and Ireland one penny per gallon.

The great dispute was concerning the power of charging Ireland by the parliament of England:

1. It was said we had the same power to charge Ireland that we have of other plantations.

2. That England has *de facto* bound Ireland as when the

16. Grey gives only three short speeches on supply.

statute enacts that Dublin and Droghedah should be statutes of the staple.[17]

3. That Ireland is a burden to us and supported by money from hence, and since we maintain it, it is but reasonable we should govern it.

4. That the act of *decimo septimo Caroli Primi*[18] did bind Ireland and dispose of the lands and estates there.

5. That the Duke of Ormonde and the Earl of Inchequin, principal persons of that kingdom, did take acts of parliament of this kingdom for the restitution of their estates there;[19] an argument they held on acts valid there.

6. That in the acts for postage and for navigation passed this parliament we have bound them.[20]

To this it was answered: That Ireland was not a plantation but a distinct kingdom governed by laws and parliament of its own; that it seemed inconsistent with the nature of a government by king, lords and commons to be charged by any other power than the parliament of that kingdom, they having no representatives in this; that we do not yet offer to tax our plantations, which is in kindness to them that they may grow up and thrive under them, and certainly Ireland is more to be cherished in all respects than either of them. That they do lie burdened with very heavy impositions, and have by acts of parliament there given the king the duties of excise and chimney money which is very heavy upon them.[21]

I said nothing on it, as conceiving I might be looked upon as an interested person, having been a commissioner for the settling of that kingdom. And besides none dared speak against the power of England to charge Ireland, and none could speak against the convenience of charging, it being plain that if they, having their beef cheaper than we, should

17. 27 Edw. II, Stat. 2, c. 1.   18. 16 Car. I, c. 33.
19. 12 Car. II, Private acts, first group, nos. 3 and 15.
20. 15 Car. II, c. 14; 13 Car. II, c. 14.
21. 14 Car. II, c. 1; 14 and 15 Car. II, c. 8, 11; 17 and 18 Car. II, c. 18 (*Irish Statutes*).

also have their salt cheaper and free from imposition, we should lose all the victualling of ships here, as in great measure we have already done by our act for banishing of their cattle.[22]

That which occurred to me then was to this purpose:

1. That it was but reasonable at least to give some time for better consideration, and not to dispose of the interest of a kingdom by a sudden vote which nobody expected nor could be prepared for.

2. That I believe they can yet show no precedent at all in the point, and that all the instances they could produce would either be:

1. Of such things as the king by his own prerogative could do, and such are the ordinances *de moneta*,[23] wherein he may bind Ireland, no doubt as well England if he will; 2. or such things as are for their advantage in which they do willingly submit and not dispute any authority by which they are benefited. Such are the statutes of making Dublin and Droghedah staple towns; such are the late statutes of navigation and of settling this post office, and such is the act of indemnity here, which was not mentioned in the House;[24] 3. or at least they are things done before they had a settled, regulated parliament there, since which time and especially since Henry VII's time when Poyning's act passed,[25] settling the manner how all acts of parliament shall pass in that kingdom has neither been offered by any prince or any parliament in England.[26] And when some such thing was agitating in par-

22. 18 and 19 Car. II, c. 2.
23. Perhaps the *Statuta de Moneta* of uncertain date (*Statutes*, I, 219) but more probably 17 Edw. IV, c. 1, and 19 Hen. VII, c. 5.
24. 12 Car. II, c. 10.
25. 10 Hen. VII, c. 4 (*Irish Statutes*).
26. Dering apparently omitted several words from this sentence. It probably should read: "since which time and especially since Poyning's act passed, settling the manner how all acts of parliament shall pass in that kingdom, *an act governing Ireland* has neither been offered by any prince or any parliament in England."

liament in Queen Elizabeth's time she sent to them expressly forbidding them to interpose in matters of Ireland.

3. That as to the private acts of the Duke of Ormonde and the Earl of Inchequin (to which may also be added the Earl of Roscommon),[27] all they had [were] either particular acts in the Irish parliament or at least promises in the act of settlement for their estates.

4. That as to the act of *decimo septimo* (*Caroli Primi*), it was said by MR. HENRY COVENTRY that that act was made in a time when that nation was wholly in rebellion; that neither parliament nor any courts of justice could then sit there, and provision must be made here or nowhere for the reducing it. And besides, the King disposing only of lands forfeited to him by that rebellion did in truth only dispose of his own, which he might well do by an act here; to which I should add that even the act of *decimo septimo* upon which so much weight is laid was never executed, nor did the King send commissioners from hence to execute it, till he upon that foundation built up another act to be passed in the parliament of Ireland, which was passed accordingly,[28] so that in truth no man holds a foot of land in Ireland by that act, nor any other of the acts passed here.

5. That it is a local opinion, all the lawyers in England holding an act of parliament here does bind Ireland if it be named, and all the lawyers and judges there holding the contrary, so that there can be little fruit of this resolution here when the duty cannot be received in the courts of Dublin.

6. That I should not presume to limit their power, which I knew to be great and might get to be much greater, but it would be no diminution of their power, nor blemish to their justice to use that power with as much moderation as our ancestors had done; and therefore to leave out Ireland out of the present question and to go on with the rest.

27. 12 Car. II, Private acts, second group, no. 3.
28. I have been unable to find any such act in the Irish statutes.

Monday [November] 28[29]

THE House went on with the report of the committee, and
agreed to most, only increasing the duty upon some sort of
silks imported from 6 to 18*d.*, and upon cable, yarn, twine,
and cordage from 8 to 18*d.* Then ordered Mr. Attorney General and Sir Robert Howard to prepare a bill for these particulars already passed, that so we might lose no time.

It was moved that 5*l.* might be set upon all horses brought
from beyond sea. This was moved by SIR GEORGE DOWNING,
to which SIR JOHN KNIGHT moved that geldings and mares
be added, which was agreeable to the House, but when it was
like to be tacked SIR THOMAS LEE* said that it was not usual
to set any imposition in the House nor to raise any money in
the House, but only at a grand committee where every body
had freedom of debate and might speak as often as they
pleased; which being agreed to be the order of the House, it
was laid aside till the committee sat.

Tuesday [November] 29[30]

THE House proceeded with several other things for the
King's supply, and resolved that Thursday, Friday, and
Saturday this week be wholly applied to that purpose, and
that after Saturday no propositions more be received.

They spent also very much of this morning about a breach
of privilege complained of by Mr. Jay, burgess for Norwich;
he had purchased the land 14 years since and had been in
quiet possession 9 years, then there was an ejectment brought
against a casual ejector, and the judgment by *nihil dicis,* and
a writ of *habere facias possessionem* upon it, whereby Mr.
Jay was turned out of possession; but this being 5 years since,

* SIR THOMAS LEE . . . *freedom of debate* underscored in MS.

29. Grey records the debates on the duties to be imposed upon French
canvasses, thrown silk, and sugar.

30. Grey reports only one speech on supply, and omits any discussion of
Jay's case.

the House would not construe it a breach of privilege, but supposed the same to be done in time of prorogation when there was no privilege. But there was also a sheepwalk or sheep ground of which Mr. Jay was dispossessed very lately, and this being in his own possession and not appearing to be comprehended within the declaration or writ of execution, was urged as a breach of privilege, but the committee had reported generally that they conceived there was no breach of privilege committed, and that the member had no cause to complain.

This being reported to the House as the opinion of the committee by SIR JOB CHARLETON, the question was whether to agree with the committee; and the House being divided upon it, it was carried in the negative, and I conceive justly, for it seems to me a plain breach of privilege as can be. Then the question was put for the recommitting of it, which was also carried in the negative, so the matter stands as it did; but the three men who had entered upon this sheepwalk were called to the Bar and told that the House were of opinion that they had committed breach of privilege against Mr. Jay, and that they expected from them they should restore the possession of the sheepwalk to him.

[Wednesday November] 30

WEDNESDAY being St. Andrews Day the House did not sit.

Thursday [December] 1[1]

THE House this day took into consideration the King's supply, and it was strongly moved it might be by a land tax, but after a very long debate it came to the question and was carried in the negative. The members of the House of both sides were $\begin{cases} 152 \\ 109. \end{cases}$

1. Grey has three pages of this debate.

Friday [December] 2[2]

THE House spent the whole day upon several proposals concerning the raising a supply for the King, and having before them several ways of a poll bill, a double poll bill, of the paper bill, of a charge upon grants and patents and other writs and processes at law, and every man speaking to which of them he would without any regularity, the whole day was spent and nothing therein done.

Saturday [December] 3[3]

THE* House in the first place thought fit to revoke their order by which no propositions for the King's supply were to be received after Saturday this day, and enlarged the time for that occasion till Tuesday next.

Then they went upon Sir Robert Howard's proposals, and he being asked what he did value the whole profit passed which might be raised by this proposal relating to the law, he said he hoped it might come to be worth 50,000 or thereabouts. Mr. Dowdeswell and Mr. Spry and some others were of opinion that it would raise 400,000, and they said this was no new proposal but the same which had been made to the House 6 years since, and then called the paper bill; that they had taken much pains in it, and had, by conference with the several officers concerned in it, computed it at 150,000l. per annum, and they did not then lay the imposition at above one 3rd of that which Sir Robert Howard had done. But the House received it and went over several paragraphs of it; they allowed and voted them all except what was upon deeds having the uses of fines and recoveries, which being often kept in private could not be taxed so properly as things upon record.

* *The House . . . Saturday this day* underscored in MS.
2. Grey has two pages of this debate.
3. Grey's account of this day's proceedings is not as full as Dering's.

Amidst this debate Mr. Garraway threw in a proposition that every person taking a dispensation to keep two livings should pay ten pounds to the King.

1. To which it was answered that this was altogether foreign to the present discourse of Sir Robert Howard's paper.

2. That this was a privilege the Lords had by the statute to qualify their chaplains to keep pluralities,[4] and therefore not likely they would pass such an act.

3. That many times livings were so poor as no man would take them singly, and therefore it was better they should have half a minister than none at all.

4. That it is fit there should be a distinction of rewards and employments as there is of abilities and merit.

5. That ten pounds was too little to reform the abuse. But the proposal being plausible the committee possessed themselves of it.

1. And nothing being answered to the first.

2. To the 2nd, it was acknowledged to be true, but it had been often attempted to be remedied and never could because such bills could never pass the Lords, but bills of money and for the King's supply seldom being refused there, it was the only way to get it passed to clap it into this bill.

3. It was agreed the ten pounds not to be paid, unless the livings together were of the value of 100*l.* per annum.

4. That there was difference already enough between livings, and if there were not, yet canonries and prebendaries were still allowable to be held together with a parsonage, but not 2 cures of souls.

5. That indeed this was much too little to hope any great reformation in that abuse, but it would at least be a mark of the parliament's aversion from pluralities, and some time or other be an occasion of looking further into it. And the committee being divided upon the question, it was carried in the affirmative.

4. 21 Hen. VIII, c. 13.

When the Speaker took his chair again it was ordered this committee should sit again on Monday and at ten of the clock, the Speaker then leaving the chair to proceed in the King's supply.

Ordered also that the House should be called over on Tuesday 13 December, and a committee made to inspect the books and journals, and to report what ways have been used to punish members neglecting to attend the house.

MR. GARRAWAY moved, and MR. WILLIAMS (alias CROMWELL) seconded it, that we should print the names of such as should be found absent, but this course I do not like, and may have very ill consequences.

THE SPEAKER informed us that the only old way he knew of was to fine the members and estreat the fines by our clerk into the exchequer.

Monday [December] 5[5]

WE proceeded again upon the King's supply. Ordered: imposition upon all foreign horses which shall be imported into England other than those of the breed of Scotland and Ireland, and that the imposition be of ten pounds apiece.

Ordered: all foreign coaches and chariots imported shall pay 50 pound apiece. Ordered: that French garments brought in ready made or ready cut out do pay 50 per cent *ad valorem* and confiscation.

Tuesday [December] 6[6]

[WE] proceeded in the King's supply. A motion made by Col. Sandys that an imposition should be raised upon all licenses granted to alehouses; none to pay less than 5*s*. nor more than 25*s*. This was long debated and at last the House divided upon it and carried in the negative.

5. Omitted in Grey.   6. Omitted in Grey.

1. Because alehouses were already taxed to the height in the old excise and in the new additional duty.

2. Because those who did speak for it seemed to intend that the commissioners who should collect this duty of licenses, should also have the power of granting the licenses, in which case the power would be wholly taken out of the justices of peace for governing them and preventing the abuses committed by them.

Then Sir John Montagu moved that there might be an imposition upon the play houses, and that every one that comes in should pay 12*d.* for the boxes, 6*d.* for the pit, 3*d.* for every other place; which at last was voted.

Wednesday [December] 7[7]

THE time enlarged to Saturday next for receiving propositions for the King's supply, with several other things which I have forgot.

[Thursday December] 8[8]

THURSDAY was spent in debate what we should further do for the King's supply, and the time enlarged to Saturday next, and the question several ways put whether we should receive propositions at all, whether we should proceed on further considerations for his Majesty's supply, or on consideration of his Majesty's further supply, or to consider the completing of his Majesty's supply.

At last, when we could not well agree in the words, Sir Job Charleton moved that we might read the order by which we had enlarged the time twice already and we might make this 3rd. enlargement in the same terms; which was agreed to.

7. Omitted in Grey.   8. Omitted in Grey.

Friday [December] 9[9]

WE began with a report from COL. BIRCH concerning the valuations of the new excise intended to be laid upon several foreign commodities, which with deductions made for such of them as were exported came to about 232,000 pounds per annum.

It was moved by Sir Thomas Clifford that for saving our time we would cast in all the 3 bills now under consideration for the King's supply and rate them together at four hundred thousand pound per annum. That is to say:

1. The additional duty upon beer and ale valued at 150,000.

2. The new duty upon foreign commodities—220,000.

3. The duty payable upon writs, and pleas, and records, etc., commonly called the paper bill—30,000.

It was much urged by Sir Robert Howard, Secretary Trevor, Sir John Duncombe, Mr. Coventry, and others that this was the highest valuation they could possibly come to:

1. For the duty upon beer and ale might possibly decrease, it being already charged as high as it can probably bear, and many doubtless would give over that profession.

2. That the duty upon foreign commodities would certainly decrease, as by all impositions it does, and then the King [would] not only lose in his new duty but in his customs also.

3. That this new duty upon foreign commodities was in truth as to many particulars imposed not to suit a revenue, but to keep out the things taxed.

4. That this estimate from the custom house was taken in 1668 which, being the year after the war with Holland, was of extraordinary affluence of trade like a stream of water which had been stopped by a dam.

5. That here was no defalcation made for damaged goods, nor for the 5 per cent and ten per cent allowed to the merchants.

9. Omitted in Grey.

6. That here was no allowance for the charge of officers necessary for the collecting it.

7. That the duties being high, much of it would be stolen.

To this was answered by Sir William Coventry, Mr. Boscawen, Sir Thomas Lee, Sir Thomas Meres, etc.:

1. That the duty upon beer and ale would certainly increase, that of London alone being set at 140,000 per annum (Middlesex and Sussex included) and that so great a pennyworth to the brewers that everyone sees the great advantage they have by it; that the country excise is said to be improvable, and that, by confession indeed, to 30,000 per annum; and it must be so, for it is now set but at 200,000 pounds per annum, whereas all England does certainly double the expense of London; that this addition is more than of one moiety of the duty because though it be but a moiety of the old duty in strong beer, yet it is an equal charge upon small beer; viz. 6*d*. per barrel, which is as much more as the former duty; that we did not hear of any person giving over either their farms or their brew-houses, but all saw what great estates those employed therein did get, it being evident that they received more by reason of this duty than they paid, and therefore that this duty of the excise might well be valued at 170,000 per annum.

2. That there was no probability the duty upon the importing foreign commodities would decrease but rather increase as it had done of late years.

3. That though some commodities were rated so high because they would discourage the importing them rather than for any desire to raise the King a supply from them, yet they were but few, and the least considerable; and that tobacco, sugar and salt, which were the principal members upon which this revenue must arise, were things which we could not want.

4. That the 4th. was a mistake, for this estimate was not taken the year after the fire of London nor presently after the peace, which was in 1667, but was from Michaelmas 1668 to Michaelmas 1669, which was a good while after the peace,

and consequently after that great glut of trade which had been stopped by the war, and therefore was the account of a year probably rather worse than better than ordinary.

5. That for defalcation on damaged goods, and of the 15 per cent allowed the merchants, there was no reason to make any abatement because that was discounted to the merchant beforehand, for damaged goods was not paid for by them nor entered in the custom house, and the 15 per cent was not to be discounted here nor would be upon the new duty.

6. That there needed no allowance for officers, for it was intended and probably would be hired by them who hired the customs, and so would be collected together.

7. That the duties being high would be attempted to be stolen, but most of it was upon gross goods which cannot be stolen; viz., sugar, salt, and tobacco; and for other goods, if there were a temptation to steal them, there is also a reward for watching them; and that the set sum of some of these uncustomed goods will answer for the escape of others; and therefore that this being worth 230,000*l.*, and the beer and ale at 170,000, they did arrive at 400,000 per annum without the paper bill; but above all, it was strongly urged that there being a committee appointed to inquire into the values of the paper bill, and they having made no return, it was very unreasonable to make yet any estimate thereof.

But it being pressed on the other side that his Majesty's wants were very great, and sudden supplies very necessary; that a return from the several officers concerned in the paper bill both here and in the country could not be had in two months' time; that it was no hurt if the bill did come to something more than 400,000 but very much if it should fall short; it was put to the question whether the paper bill should be cast in to make up 400,000 per annum. And the committee being divided upon it it was carried in the affirmative, and, though the reason was very strong against casting in the paper bill into a certain sum before we had an estimate made of it by a report from the committee, yet the House having already voted that the paper bill should be part of his Majesty's supply, and it being my opinion that the other two bills were not of the value of 400,000*l*. per annum, I went in the affirmative, for though it may now be really worth 450,000*l*. per annum, yet since the other two were not sufficient without it, there was a necessity of making it up by this third.

Saturday [December] 10[10]

HIS Majesty in the morning sent for the House to Whitehall, and there informed them that the French King had by his ambassador here acquainted him that he intended to come to Dunkirk this summer with 40,000 foot, but it was only to discipline his men and repair his fortifications, and not to trouble or invade any of his neighbors; that he thought fit to tell them of it, to let them see the necessity of being well prepared, that we might owe our safety to our own strength, and not to his courtesy; and mentioned to them the providing of 800,000*l*. ready money which would enable him to set out his fleet this summer, and if this were done he did hope he should not call upon them for money a great while, but that the next session might be only to provide good laws for the people, and not be spent in providing supplies for him.

THE SPEAKER returning in to the House reported the effect of his Majesty's speech, and presently SIR FRETCHVILLE HOLLIS moved for a poll bill; MR. WILLIAMS, alias CROMWELL, moved for a year's rent from all the new buildings about London which would bring into the King 600,000.

This motion was seconded by SIR NICHOLAS CARY, and was likely if it had been presented to have taken up much of this day which was the last designed for the King's supply.

But it being then urged that we should take the King's speech to us into consideration and think of the present danger from France; this was much reflected upon by others as not proper for us to take notice of at all, [it being] not likely

10. Omitted in Grey.

to be the King of France's intentions since [they were] discovered to us by his own ambassador, not by any intelligence of ours; and if this might be said, then whenever the King of France would send us word he would come to our coast, he must put us to the charge of 800,000; which would make us not only poor but ridiculous also.

It was answered that the matter was of importance enough, and whatsoever the King of France did promise, it was not good nor prudent to see an enemy armed at our door, and not to find ourselves in a posture of defense; that though we did not believe what the French ambassador said, yet it was a favor from his Majesty to acquaint us with what intelligence he had received, especially since his Majesty did not urge us from thence to any further supply than what before this he had desired, which was 800,000, and which was absolutely necessary to setting forth his fleet.

The debt due from his Majesty to the Prince of Orange was also mentioned, and the great merits of that family toward the King in his banishment. This was pressed by SIR WILLIAM COVENTRY, MR. HENRY COVENTRY, and MR. WALLER, but took no effect, it being unseasonable and not at all recommended to us or desired of us by the King. But that which took up the whole debate of the day was whether we should debate of the King's supply and the raising of ready money in the House or in the grand committee.

It was said that it* is a standing order of the House that all supplies of money shall be debated in a grand committee where everyone might speak as often as he would and not be tied up to once; that this manner was affirmed by an express order made last year in this House upon search of precedents and report of a committee appointed to this purpose;[11] that there is an express order made yesterday that the House shall resolve into a grand committee this day for this supply.[12]

---

* *It is a standing order . . . in a grand committee* underscored in MS.
11. Feb. 18, 1667–8 (*C.J.* IX, 52).
12. No such order appears in the *Journal*.

These two orders were desired to be read, and the reading of them a long time was opposed but at last consented to by the House without dividing, and surely with much reason, it being an undoubted thing that any* member may demand the reading of an order made by the House in the matter then in debate.

But this being granted, although the orders were full to the purpose, yet it was said that it was no infringement to these orders for the House to give some instructions to the committee before they sat; that this was very useful, for if the House were of opinion a small sum would supply the King, then one sort of proposals should serve; if the sum were great then proposals of another nature must be made.

About two of the clock the question was put whether any further instructions should be given the grand committee before they entered upon the King's supply, and the House being divided, the affirmatives were 123, the negatives 109.[13]

When this was carried, then the next consideration was what instructions should be given them.

1. And it was strongly urged that the† *quantum* nor the *modus* of any imposition was never yet resolved in the House before it had been debated in a grand committee.

2. And that to vote a sum certain would be to induce upon us again the necessity of a land tax, nothing else being of any certainty for a precise sum.

It was answered that for a land tax they would consent the question should be put with an exclusion thereof, and for a certain sum; they desired it should be put only near‡ 800,000.

The other side going off from their first point (in which I take it they were in the right) desired the question might be for raising a sum not exceeding 800,000, and after a long debate, at past 4 the question was stated whether the grand

* *Any member . . . then in debate* underscored in MS.
† *The* quantum *. . . in a grand committee* underscored in MS.
‡ *Near 800,000* underscored in MS.
13. In the *Journal* (IX, 181) the division is recorded as 128 to 112.

committee should consider of a further supply for the King which should be about and not exceeding 800,000, and the question being put if the word "about" should be part of the question, the House divided and the affirmatives were 128 and the negatives 116.[14]

Monday December 12[15]

AT the first sitting of the House several private bills were read and committed; one for confirming an agreement between the Lord Stafford and his tenants, and one for confirming some leases and raising of portions of 4,000 apiece for the two daughters of Sir Clifford Clifton.

Then the Speaker left the chair, and the House resolved into a grand committee to consider the King's supply. And it being moved among other things that it was possible to supply the King out of his own, and that there was a million of money yet due the King of the former aids given him since his coming in, and this was in the receiver's hands, and it was just to fetch it from thence rather than to draw more from the people, it was answered that it was not credible such a vast sum nor indeed any great sum did remain in the collectors' hands or receivers'; that if did, it was desperate not to be gotten at all, much less in so speedy a way as the King's occasions did require, and that at most this was not to give the King any new supply, but to tell him of his own, and what his officers already knew much better than we; that all this that was in arrears was already charged and assigned to men for the King's debts, and if it were recovered, must go to that use, and not to furnishing the navy as this 800,000 lately voted is designed.

After this Sir George Downing, taking upon him to give an account of what is owing to the King by the receivers, said

14. In the *Journal* (IX, 181) the division is recorded as 124 to 111.
15. Grey reports only a short debate on the nature of subsidies.

there was not standing out in all above 110,000*l.*; that of this 110,000, 25,000 was due from the City of London, which by reason of the calamity of the fire was yet respited; much of the rest, process was gone out for, and there was a consider- able part of* the rest which was owing by members of the House who were not proceeded against by reason of their privilege.

These last words gave great offense to the House, and it was urged that it was a reflection upon the whole House that members should sit there to vote away the people's money and then to keep it themselves when they had done; that it was hoped there was none such or but few; and that he should name the persons.

And it was ordered presently that the Speaker should resume the chair that then Sir George Downing might name the persons, or if he could not, he should be sent to the Tower for the scandal he had raised.

The Speaker resuming the chair, the matter was aggra- vated very much by some, and extenuated and defended by others. At last being required peremptorily to name them at his peril, he desired time till the next day to search into his papers, that so he might do it more exactly and satisfactorily than he could do upon his memory. But it being not satisfac- tory to the House, and it being said that it was not necessary he should name the sums, nor likely he should forget the names of the persons; and the motion of sending him to the Tower being again renewed, at last he named four:

1. SIR JOHN PRETTYMAN, who rose up in his place and denied that he owed the King anything.

2. MAJOR WALDEN of Huntingdonshire, who acknowl- edged he owed the King money, but that there was as much (or very near) owing to him by Sir Dennis Gourden, victual- ler of the navy, and that he was petitioning his Majesty that one account might balance the other.

* *Of the rest . . . of their privilege* underscored in MS.

3. COLONEL GILBY, who did not in truth owe anything to the King but is security for one that does.

4. Colonel Harlachendon in Kent, who is indebted to his Majesty 1,700*l.*, and for whom nothing was said, he being absent himself.

The House thought this a very small account for so great an imputation, and therefore ordered him to bring in a fuller account tomorrow morning, with the sums also that were owing. They ordered also the commissioners of Brook House to give an account of what money they find owing upon the several aids given to his Majesty.

After this the House resolved again into a committee to consider of the King's supply, and after several propositions for the new buildings for to lay it upon the Jews,[16] and some other things very remote, at last the House resolved that his Majesty's supply should be raised by a pound rate according to the true yearly value of all lands and offices, and by a rate also upon money and goods.

Tuesday [December] 13[17]

THE House began with reading a long tedious bill brought in by SIR ROBERT STEWARD for regulating of servants' wages, and in going into many things very improper for a bill of that title. It was the sense of the House to cast it quite out, but being told by THE SPEAKER that if we should put it to question and* it be cast out, we could not bring in any other bill for that purpose this session; and it being against the sense of the House to give this bill a second reading, it was moved by MR. CROUCH as an expedient that Sir Robert Steward might have† leave to withdraw this bill and to bring in

---

* *And it be cast out . . . that purpose this session* underscored in MS.
† *Have leave . . . no such order might be made* underscored in MS.
16. See below, p. 70.
17. Grey gives only a brief account of the members named by Downing.

another better penned, and confined wholly to the matter of servants' wages; which was approved of.

But MR. HAMDEN moved the House that no such order might be made, there being no precedent that any bill of which the House was possessed and which had been once read was ever withdrawn by order; and the consequence of it might be that a bill which was likely to miscarry upon a full debate might have leave to be withdrawn, and then be tendered again at some more favorable opportunity, and therefore when such things were done it was only by connivance of the House and not by order, and this was well approved by the House.

Then they ordered a committee to bring in a bill for regulating servants' wages, taking no notice of the bill they now had. And they added they should take consideration also of employing the poor, without which the servants could not be governed.

SIR THOMAS LEE moved that none might depart without certificate from their former master or from a justice of peace if his master should refuse.

COLONEL BIRCH that a stock might be raised for employing the poor.

SIR RICHARD BARNES for regulating the apparel of servants, all which was received to the care of the committee.

SIR THOMAS HIGGONS moved that as an expedient to make servants more tractable we might bring into this kingdom the use of Negro slaves, but this was not relished by the House nor seconded by any.

After this business done they called upon SIR GEORGE DOWNING, who to his former list of 4 now added about 4 more; viz.:

1. MR. WALTER STRICKLAND, who confessed he owed the King 2,000, but said the King owed him as much upon a former grant, which he hoped would balance it.

2. COLONEL PRICE of Herefordshire, who said the money was ready.

3. COL. KIRBY, who was indebted about 500.

4. And a fourth whom I have forgot.[18]

After this the commissioners of Brook House were called in, who brought in their accounts; viz., Col. Thompson, Colonel Osborne, Sir James Langham, and two others whom I know not. The account they gave in of arrears was about 270,000, but this account was made up in August 1669, and the truth is that much the greatest part of this money is paid in since, and some remains yet unpaid, and some in subcollectors' hands in the country.

Upon the whole matter the House were satisfied that there was no great matter to be expected from all this information of any advantage to the King, and that what could be got would certainly be brought in by the exchequer process.

So they left off further consideration thereof, and then it was moved and urged that to vindicate ourselves from this aspersion of keeping the King's money in our hands it is fit the House should humbly petition the King that henceforth no member of parliament should be employed by him as receivers of any part of the aid or supplies which shall be given him.

This was as much opposed because it was not a vindication of ourselves, but a reflection that we were not fit to be trusted; that the greatest part of the receivers had discharged their trust very well; that if those who are yet in arrears have yet satisfied the House that there was not reason enough for the information against them, that most of them were suffering and meriting persons, and if some tenderness were used toward them, it was not to be blamed; that the King might employ whom he thought fit, and it was not reasonable to limit him in his choice.

And the question at last being put whether such address should be made to the King it was carried in the negative.

18. Grey's account is more categorical; see I, 322–3.

We had besides a very long debate concerning the taxes still in arrears, how they should be got in, and what to do with those which are really insolvent; and the case was laid before us of the county of Suffolk, in which the high collector for Ipswich division is run away with 5,000*l.*; it seemed very hard the county who had paid it should be reassessed, and THE SPEAKER told us the judges had resolved it could not so be done by the law. It seemed hard also that the King should lose it, it being given him by act of parliament and cannot be taken away but by act; and the high collector being named not by the King, there is no reason it should be at the King's hazard. There remains then only that the commissioners of that county should make it good, and then the question is whether all the commissioners of that county, or all the commissioners of that division—there being three divisions in which the commissioners act severally—or only those commissioners which named him. And it seemed hard that the commissioners in the other divisions should be concerned at all, the act requiring them to act in their several divisions. And it is not very reasonable that gentlemen who are trusted to act for the King and country and named by act of parliament, most of them without their seeking, and who act at their own charge without any manner of benefit or salary, shall be liable to make good the miscarriage of others. And yet the act requiring the commissioners to take security of the high collector that they be responsible, and to inspect their accounts every 3 months (as I take it), there must certainly have been some remissness in these commissioners which may be charged upon them.

This case of Suffolk is now depending in the exchequer between the King and the commissioners, and by what was said, one might conjecture the opinion of the King's counsel to be that all the commissioners of that county are liable unto this debt. But the House came to no resolution in it, but appointed a committee to sit upon it.

Wednesday December 14[19]

THE House began with a private bill to confirm a sale of land made by John Coplestone of Devonshire to Hugh Stafford, but there being a marriage settlement and an infant in the case, and nothing appearing of any reason to induce the House to it, they cast it out upon the first reading, which is the first they have served so a good while.

Then we went upon completing the King's supply, and for a long time the discourse went upon the quantity of acres or of values of England, some saying it was 18, some 12, some but 9 millions yearly; some that it was 50, some 36, some 30, some but 24 millions of acres.

Some computed that since 2s. per pound did raise 70,000 per mensem, which is 840,000 in one year, then 12d. per pound would raise 420,000.

Others saying that to the tax of 70,000 per mensem Cheshire and some other counties did not pay above 5d. per pound, and therefore 12d. per pound at the true full value would raise the whole sum of 80,000.

The most probable calculation I could hear was that the revenue of the Kingdom was about 12 millions per annum, the consequence whereof is that 12d. per pound of the true yearly value is 600,000.

Much was said that a subsidy of a penny per pound would raise 100,000, and therefore we might give eight subsidies, to have them paid at four payments.

But at last Mr. Garraway moved that we were out of the way, and that it was necessary to consider first what to lay upon money, goods, and offices, before we came to lay anything at all upon lands, which had born the burden all along; and the measure of lands, and the estimate we can make of them being something more probable than any account we yet

19. Grey's report of this debate is less full than Dering's.

have of the rest, it is fit to examine first what the rest will
bear, that so we may supply it by a charge upon the land.

Upon this we fell into a debate concerning charging of
money, and it was moved that all money should pay ten shillings for every hundred pounds. It was desired by myself
and others that the word "at interest" should be added to the
question, for it may seem very reasonable that money which
produces profit should also pay towards the King's supply,
but for money which made no profit and peradventure never
should, there was no reason to charge it; and how unfitting
is it if a man, when this act shall take effect, shall have a
100*l.* by him for his necessary expense, or if a gentleman
have then received 500 for his half year's rent may if his
tenant have but provided it, and beg to pay it to his landlord
within a week following, or a merchant who is going with it
in his hand to pay for wares, all this money must yet pay to
the King. And at last, how shall this money which is con-
cealed and buried, be ever found out to be taxed?

However, after all, the sense of the House was to tax all
money whether at interest or not at interest, and so it passed:
to pay 10*s.* every 100*l.* to the King.

It was then moved that all in the bankers' hands might pay
15*s.* per cent.

Much was said in their defense, some that it would ruin
them absolutely; some that what we should get from them
was an inconsiderable sum and not worth the taking notice
of, and so perhaps it is, but the House were so incensed
against their rating interest at 10 per cent of the King that
they resolved to put some discountenance upon them, and resolved, the committee being divided upon it, that 15*s.* per
cent should be paid out of all money in the hands of the
bankers.

Then they proceeded to vote that money may be lent to the
King upon the security of this act at 7 per cent interest and
that also such money as should so be lent to his Majesty
should not be taxed towards his supply but discharged of the

10s. per cent other money is liable to. This is done in hope to draw all the money out of the bankers' hands, supposing that all people will rather lend the King at 7 per cent than the banker at 6; and if the bankers will transfer their debts which they have upon the other branches of the revenue, and place them upon this to save the 15s. per cent then the King's revenue shall presently be cleared, and he will immediately save 3 per cent.

Then we proceeded to tax all stock employed in trade and this was much opposed by the merchants, but these were 2 reasons offered which they did not answer:

1. That we had resolved this already, since we had voted goods should be taxed, for the word "money" would not comprehend it, and if it did, then they must pay as money, which would be too much.

2. That in all taxes formerly used, and in all subsidies, goods were ever taxed, and when* lands were taxed at four shillings the pound, goods were always taxed at 8 groats.

So we proceeded to the vote, and resolved that all stock in trade should pay at the rate of 6s. the hundred pound. We resolved that stock upon land and household stuff shall not be taxed.

Then the Speaker took the chair, and MR. SEYMOUR asked leave for this committee to sit again tomorrow morning upon the same business.

Then leave was asked for Mr. Mallet to go down into the country, his wife being sick, but between jest and earnest he could not get leave.

Memo: Sir Thomas Gower said that Doomsday Book had made 60,000 knights' fees, and every fee was 6 hides of land, and every hide 100 acres; by which computation he swells the number of acres beyond any account I have ever heard.[20] He said also that in Henry VI's time the commissioners were

* *When lands . . . at 8 groats* underscored in MS.

20. The number 60,000 (first mentioned by Ordericus Vitalis) represents the true number of knights' fees multiplied by more than ten. The number

upon oath, and had power to give an oath to others, and if it appeared the person had undervalued his estate and that proved by oath, then he was to pay treble.

Thursday [December] 15[21]

THE House began with reading a bill brought in by COLONEL BIRCH for making one standing measure for corn and salt throughout the kingdoms, by which it is enacted they should be all measured by a seated brass measure, which seated measure should be had here in London, and bought by all corporations and market towns; and it enacts that nobody should shake their corn or salt, and some other unreasonable things; but the bill was committed to be amended.

Then we proceeded in a grand committee to complete the King's supply, and the first question was concerning stock in trade. Therein it was resolved that allowance and deductions be made for so much as was owing by the tradesman, for that no more was truly his own than what remained when his debt was paid.

Then we proceeded to tax officers, and it was moved by Sir Jonathan Trelawny, and seconded by Sir Thomas Clifford, that all officers should pay 2s. per pound of the yearly values or income.

It was urged that there was no reason to tax offices higher than lands, no office being for more than a man's life, most of them being indeed but during the King's pleasure and therefore in no sort equal to an inheritance; that all offices had been taxed ever since the King's coming in equal with lands and so had their share of the burden, and had besides one tax particularly upon them, which was not upon lands, which was that for the supply of the indigent loyal officers. Sir Jonathan Trelawny, Sir Thomas Clifford, Mr. Lawrence Hyde, Mr.

of hides in each fee varied considerably. (J. H. Round, *Feudal England,* pp. 290–295.)

21. Grey's report of this debate is less full than Dering's.

Garraway, Mr. Weld spoke for it; Sir John Ernle, Sir Charles Harbord, Mr. Boscawen, Sir John Bramston, and others spoke against it as highly unequal, and the committee divided upon it, and it was carried they should be taxed with 2s. the pound.

Then we proceeded upon what remained to complete the King's supply, which was a pound rate upon the lands according to the full value. Much controversy was between the rates of 8d. per pound and 12d. per pound, and truly by computation 8d. per pound could not probably make up the sum voted of 800,000, for the account is stated several ways, and many had taken pains therein, but their calculations were very different.

At half an hour past two the question was put for 12d. per pound, and the affirmatives were 103, the negatives 97, in all 200.

The most probable estimate:

1. That the current money of the nation is not above 12 millions, which at 10s. every 100l. will make but 60,000.

2. That the stock in trade, deducting for debts and household stuffs, and stock upon land, which are not to be taxed, is not above 25 millions of pounds, which at 6s. the hundred pound will produce but 75,000.

3. That the officers at 2s. every hundred pound revenue will not produce above 24,000.

4. That the full yearly value of all the rest of lands and houses in England is not above 12 millions, which at twelve pence in the pound does produce just 600,000.

Tuesday December 20[22]

THE House having received the intimation of his Majesty's pleasure by SECRETARY TREVOR adjourned from this day to Thursday the 29th of December. Before they adjourned they ordered the House to be called over upon the 9th of January,

22. December 16, 17, and 19 are omitted by Dering. December 20 is omitted by Grey.

and all absent members to pay double subsidy and to be put into the act by name, and that the Speaker send his letters to the several sheriffs in England and Wales to give notice thereof to the respective members.

[Thursday] December 29

THE House met according to order but immediately adjourned to Tuesday the 3rd of January.

[Tuesday] January 3[1]

THE House met and read the bill for the King's subsidy for raising the 800,000 the first time, and ordered the reading of it again upon that day seven night.

[Wednesday] January 4[2]

THE House met, and read the bill for the new excise upon foreign commodities the first time, and ordered the bill to be read the second time upon Thursday the 12th of January.

Thursday January 5[3]

WE read the bill for the additional duty upon ale and beer, and ordered it to be read again this day fortnight. These two bills were brought in by SIR ROBERT HOWARD, the first by THE ATTORNEY GENERAL.

Memo: Then we read an engrossed bill for continuance of two bills made this parliament; the one for setting a price upon coals in London, the other for extents upon statutes staple.

Upon the reading, the sense of the House went generally for continuing that act for statutes staple, but not for con-

---

1. Omitted in Grey.   2. Omitted in Grey.
3. Omitted in Grey.

tinuing that for setting price upon coals; as having found by
experience that setting of prices does but make things dearer
by the scarcity where the plenty would make them cheap if
there were no restraint upon the selling them.

But the difficulty upon us was how this might be cured, for
to recommit the bill after the third reading and so to have it
amended was affirmed by THE SPEAKER to be regular and
parliamentary, and he quoted Mr. Lambarde's book in the
case,[4] and with him agreed SIR CHARLES HARBORD.

SIR JOB CHARLETON and others denied that this could be
done, and it seemed to me that it could not be, for what should
become of it after this recommitment, since it had been read
already three times; and to read it four times was altogether
irregular; and so would it be also to pass it after the recommitment without reading it again; and the consequence of it
seemed very great and dangerous to recommit engrossed bills,
which being then once put to the question must be either
passed or rejected; nor did* we ever remember that any bill
after the 3rd reading was ever so much as respited or laid
upon the table, much less recommitted, but took its fate immediately, either to pass or be rejected. The second expedient
was to amend it at the table, which is usual, but then it is only
in a word or two, something that may be done by the clerk
immediately at the table without defacing the roll, whereas
this was to strike out almost half the bill, and so to make a
hiatus and chasm very unfit to be sent up to the Lords. The
3rd way proposed was to let the bill be rejected and then to
bring in a new short bill for the particular which the House
did approve, leaving out that which they disliked. But this
was as irregular as any of the rest, it being a constant rule
that when a bill is rejected, no other bill can be brought in to

---

* *Did we ever . . . or be rejected* underscored in MS.
4. William Lambarde, *The Orders, Proceedings, Punishments, and Privileges of the Commons-House of Parliament in England* (1641), chap. VIII.
(This copy is corrupt, as is the one printed in the *Harleian Miscellany*. The
best presentation of the work is in Add. MS. 5123. See J. S. Neale, "Peter
Wentworth," *English Historical Review*, XXXIX, 50 n.)

the same effect the same session. And to lay this bill aside without a question and to bring in another new one was as bad, since we could not bring in a new bill by order while we had one depending, before brought in by order also for the same matter.

After much tossing to and fro, we at last resolved to amend it at the table as subject to less inconvenience than any of the other ways, and so it was done.

Memo: I never knew any recommitment of an engrossed bill, but it must be amended at the table or else thrown out; but I have known sometimes that when a bill has been agreed upon to be amended at the table if the amendment were difficult, and could not readily be worded to the satisfaction of the House, 3 or 4 members have been ordered to withdraw and to word it according to the sense of the House, and they having agreed, and the House approved, the amendments were then made at the table.

Then the House adjourned till Monday.

Monday January 9[5]

THE House was called over according to former order, and after all those who appeared had answered to their names the defaulters were called over again, but the House would not take the excuses which were offered then, but ordered Monday next to consider of the punishing the absent; and they were inclined to this delay because they were informed of several persons who were upon the way, but it being Monday and so immediately after Christmas and in the sessions weeks, many would doubtless be here in a little time.

The absentees were 190, so reckoning the whole number of the House to be 509, those that were present were 319.

Then the House voted to proceed tomorrow upon consideration of the horrid act committed upon the person of Sir John Coventry, a member of this House, who the day of our recess

5. Omitted in Grey.

before Christmas, going very late from supper at the Cock to his house in Suffolk Street, was set upon by about 16 men, horse and foot, wounded, and his nose barbarously and villainously cut with a knife.

Tuesday January 10[6]

THE House entered upon the debate of Sir John Coventry's business, SIR THOMAS CLERGES first giving us an account of the fact as it had appeared before him, who took the examinations upon oath as a justice of peace, by which it appears that divers of them were of the King's Life Guard, of which Mr. Lake, Wroth, Parry, and Heenes were named, and Sir Thomas Sands, and Captain Charles O'Brian, second son to the Earl Inchequin; the first two being in Newgate for the fact, the 4 last being fled; he added further that they had acquainted the lord chief justice with the examinations, who told them that the prisoners were not bailable by law, and that after they had waited upon the secretaries of state, and told them the chief justice his opinion, and the secretaries had informed them it was his Majesty's pleasure that the law should have its true course against all that were guilty of the fact.

Then SIR JOHN HOTHAM began with an invective against the thing, but moved not what to do in it, but only to wreak our vengeance upon the assassins that had done this foul and horrid act.

This was seconded in the same manner by SIR ROBERT HOLT.

THE EARL OF ANCRAM spoke to the purpose that it was a crime against the law, and that the law would give sufficient reparations.

SIR EDMUND WYNDHAM informed the House that the proceeding at law was already begun, and that it was likely to be severe enough upon them who had to do in it, it having being already found felony by the grand jury. (Memo: The

6. Grey's and Dering's reports of this debate are similar.

felony is in respect of Sir John Coventry's sword and periwig, which were taken away.)

But this did not seem to satisfy the House because this at most could but reach those who were in hold; that the principal actors were fled and so could not be reached by the common course of law, whereupon SIR JOHN MONSON moved for a bill of banishment against those which were fled, unless they came in by a short day to be prefixed by proclamation.

MR. HALE of Hertfordshire seconded that motion, MR. GARRAWAY thirded it, SIR ROBERT ATKINS fourthed it, and added that we should enquire further who were the authors, councillors and contrivers of it, and upon what ground or provocation and added that we should meddle with no other business till this bill were passed.

Hitherto we had been all unanimous, no one man offering to excuse, or so much as to extenuate the barbarous fact, and SIR WILLIAM COVENTRY and HENRY COVENTRY, uncles to Sir John Coventry, moved also for the bill of banishment, and the whole House seemed unanimously to consent to it. But upon these words of laying aside all other business, that is to say all bills of supply to the King of which there was extraordinary haste, the House entered into a great dispute, the whole subject of the debate being whether we should stop all other business or not.

For stopping were: SIR NICHOLAS CARY, SIR THOMAS LEE, SIR THOMAS MERES, SIR TREVOR WILLIAMS, MR. JONES of the city, LORD CASTLETON, SIR PHILLIP MOUNTAIN, MR. GARRAWAY, SIR THOMAS LEE, SIR THOMAS MERES, MR. WHORWOOD, SIR JOHN COTTON, SIR JOHN ERNLE, LORD CAVENDISH, MR. VAUGHAN, MR. BOSCAWEN, SIR ELIAB HARVEY, SIR JOHN KNIGHT, COLONEL BIRCH.

Against stopping were: SIR FRANCIS GOODRICK, SIR THOMAS CLIFFORD, LORD O'BRIAN, SIR THOMAS LITTLETON, SIR RICHARD TEMPLE, LORD RICHARDSON, SIR JOHN DUNCOMBE, SIR WINSTON CHURCHILL, MR. SEYMOUR, SIR SOLOMON SWALE, SIR ROBERT HOWARD, SIR FRETCHVILLE HOL-

LIS, SIR JOHN TREVOR, MR. WALLER, SIR GEORGE DOWNING, MR. TREASURER, MR. ATTORNEY GENERAL, MR. TITUS, MR. HENRY COVENTRY.

Of those who had spoke against stopping, those who spoke last did most of them consent to the thing, which they might manage well enough, having all the money bills still in their hand, which they need not send away till this bill of banishment were perfected; and indeed the bills for money were so long and subject to such exceptions, that it was impossible they could dispatch any one in 14 days. Whereas this bill for banishment being short, and carried on by unanimous consent may well be dispatched in 4 days, and therefore some moved that the bills might go on *pari passu;* some that we might sit every morning on the bills of supply, and every afternoon on the bill of banishment, and at last that they would be content to give the bill of banishment a preference, but not to vote to meddle with nothing else till that be done.

But nothing would satisfy the House but an absolute vote that no other business should be proceeded in at all while this bill of banishment was passing; and that seeming to be the sense of the House, we came to word the question; and it being moved that before the question put, we should add to it these words, "passing this House," that so we might not be bound to sit still while the bill should be in the Lord's House, which would be a strange indecency in as to sit still it may be for a week or more, and as unfitting it was to impose this upon the King and the Lords that till this bill was passed, we would not consider the King's supply nor the kingdom's ne-cessities; and if the Lords should not pass it, as they would have little reason to do coming to them upon such peremptory terms, we could proceed no further, but the parliament must end; and the Lords may as well send us down a bill and say they will do nothing till that is passed; and when bills do stick in either House we can send up messages to quicken them, or we may demand a conference with them concerning it; and that in effect this was as great a breach of privilege upon the Lords, as this affront done to Sir John Coventry was of ours. And now the debate ran very warm whether we should stop while the bill was passing our own House or till it passed the Lords also.

For passing both Houses: SIR THOMAS LEE, MR. CHEYNEY, SIR NICHOLAS CARY, SIR THOMAS MERES, MR. GARRAWAY.

For passing only our House: SIR ROBERT HOWARD, MR. MILWARD, SIR RICHARD TEMPLE, SIR CHARLES HARBORD, SIR ROBERT CARR, MR. SWINFIN.

Resolved: that a bill be brought in for banishment of those that were guilty of the assault upon Sir John Coventry, and are now fled from justice, unless they shall render themselves within a day to be prefixed; with a clause of mercy to such as shall make discovery of the actors therein, they not being the principal actors themselves; and that no other business be proceeded in while this bill is passing this House.

Then Sir William Coventry, Sir Robert Atkins, Mr. Garraway, Sir Thomas Meres, and three or four more were named a committee to bring in a bill for this purpose tomorrow morning, and all other committees were adjourned.

Wednesday [January] 11[7]

THE bill concerning Sir John Coventry was brought in by SIR THOMAS LEE, and read, and the House immediately adjourned.

[Thursday January] 12[8]

THE bill concerning Sir John Coventry was read the second time and immediately committed to a committee of the whole house, and Mr. Coleman put in the chair.

The business of the bill as far as it concerned Sir John Coventry was agreed by one of the clock, and then Sir Thomas

7. Grey's and Dering's reports of this day's debate are similar.
8. Omitted in Grey.

Meres tendered a clause for preventing like mischiefs for the time to come, which was to this effect, that whosoever should from the 16th day of February, 1670 wound, maim, or bruise any member of either House of parliament during the time of their attendance upon the parliament, it should be felony without clergy in them, their counsellors, aids, and abettors.

Much was said against this clause; that it should not be felony without clergy; much that it was not fit to restrain it only to members of parliament; but the greatest debate was that it was more proper to be a bill by itself than a part of this:

1. Because this was a particular occasion only concerning Sir John Coventry, which was fully resented by the bill before us.

2. Because this additional clause, which was very disputable, would certainly delay, and probably hazard the bill for punishing the assassination committed upon Sir John Coventry, which we did all agree in, and probably would find a clear and speedy passage with the Lords.

3. That if we did proceed to add this clause to this bill we must delay Sir John Coventry's bill which we did all desire to expedite, and thereby also delay all the bills of supply which did require haste; and also we must, to speed them, huddle up this clause with more haste than was fitting in a matter which concerned the laws and fortunes of the people whom we represented.

At 4 of the clock it came to a question whether this matter of preventing such like mischiefs for the future should be added to this bill, or in a bill by itself.

For the adding it to this bill were 85; for a distinct bill were 78.

Friday January 13[9]

THIS clause of Sir Thomas Meres was brought into the House but amended and altered from what it was, and by the House referred to the committee of the whole house.

9. Grey's report of this day's activities is much fuller than Dering's.

Whereupon the Speaker left the chair, and Mr. Coleman taking it, the committee proceeded upon the clause and agreed it with some amendments, and ordered it to be engrossed against tomorrow morning.

Saturday January 14[10]

THE bill engrossed was read, and passed, and sent up to the Lords by Sir Thomas Lee.

Then it was moved to go on presently with the bill for 800,000, but that was not ready upon the table.

The House resolved, according to former order, to call over the defaulters on Monday morning and then to proceed immediately upon the bill for 800,000.

Monday [January] 16[11]

WE proceeded, according to order, upon calling over the defaulters, of which some were excused, others, and most, their excuses were not allowed. Then we made another vote that the House should be called over again on the 31st of January, and that nobody should depart without leave under the same penalties which are now upon defaulters.

Then we entered upon the subsidy bill which being read over at length, then it was moved it might be committed as is usual, this being the second reading. This was opposed first by SIR TREVOR WILLIAMS, then by MR. JONES of London, who were for casting out the bill; and SIR TREVOR WILLIAMS moved that instead of this supply, the chimney money might be sold outright. MR. GARRAWAY and SIR THOMAS MERES and divers others spoke not to the casting out but to the laying it aside till we could consider if some better way might be proposed; which SIR THOMAS MERES undertook to do.

After a long debate the question was put for committing it; the affirmatives were 170, the negatives were 109.

10. Omitted in Grey.

11. Grey gives a full report of this day's debate, but does not mention the points of procedure.

I were in the affirmative, it being most proper, and almost constant; and though it be undoubtedly true that the House has power to cast out a bill at the first, second, or third reading, yet it is very unusual when the matter of the bill has been first voted by the House, then the manner referred to a committee of the whole house, and by these approved, there after a long debate agreed and by them approved, and a bill ordered then to be brought in to that purpose, which is done and read the first and second time, then to cast it out without committing it. For as for the matter the House has already approved it, and for the manner it ought not now to be rejected, because that may be mended by the committee, and I believe there is hardly one precedent where a bill has been cast out before it was committed which came in with all these circumstances.

Tuesday [January] 17[12]

WE read a bill concerning fencing of woods and maintaining timber, and then committed it.

At ten of the clock we entered upon the bill of subsidy, the House resolving into a grand committee, and Mr. Seymour taking the chair.

The first paragraph we entered upon after the bill read over, and the preamble postponed as is usual, was whether the charge of 10s. per cent should be paid by all money or only for money at interest, and resolved the words "at interest" should be added. Then we entered upon the clause concerning the bankers, and after a long dispute we could come to no conclusion, but desired 5 or 6 of our number to withdraw and bring in the clause amended according to the debate of the House.

Memo:* We could not order them in the committee to report tomorrow morning because we could not be sure to sit

---

* This whole paragraph underscored in MS.
12. Omitted in Grey.

tomorrow, not having order from the House to do so; and the House could not order the committee to report tomorrow because they can take no notice of what is done in the committee till they have a report, but we might order them to withdraw and to word one clause without appointing them a time to bring it in, for that is supposed to be done during the sitting of the committee.

Wednesday [January] 18[13]

WE postponed the clause concerning the bankers, and we spent the whole day upon consideration whether there should be a clause for transferring the debts his Majesty now owes upon this subsidy bill or not. Much was said [how] convenient it would be to clear his Majesty's standing revenue, which would then come in to him by constant monthly payments, whereas this would not be money at all sooner till midsummer next; and of the reasonableness to fine the bankers to part with their past security and to take to this. Others were of another mind; that we should not compel, but only invite men by the advantage of 7 per cent, of the certainty of the payment, [there] being security by act of parliament, and by the excusing them from being taxed for any money they shall so lend.

I were against any transferring at all, for to compel people was unjust, who had a better security already in their hand, and would doubtless lessen the King's credit if any emergency should occur to require it. To invite people was inconvenient, for all those who had good security for short and speedy payments would refuse to come in, and all those creditors of his Majesty who now had no interest at all, or but 6 per cent, or who were charged very remote, or were placed

13. Dering has confused January 18 and 19. The debate on supply which Dering reports on the 18th actually occurred on the 19th, and the debate on the Devonshire election, reported by Dering on the 19th, took place on the 18th. Grey reports the same debates but less fully.

upon such branches of the revenue as are overcharged, all these would come in immediately, and so this bill, which is intended to produce ready money, should be immediately swallowed up with old debts already provided for; and as it is unjust to remove them who have now a better security, so it is unreasonable to remove them hither who have lent their money upon a worse security; let them take it every man as they have it. And for the advantage of clearing the King's standing revenue by engaging this, it is not much matter, for if this be free, either men will lend upon it and then it will be ready money sooner than his revenue, or if no man will lend money upon it, yet it will of itself come in at mid-summer next, and so quarterly for all the year.

After a very long debate we waived the particulars, and came to a general question whether there should be a clause for transferring debts or not in this bill, and the committee dividing upon it, it was carried in the affirmative. But it was carried that it should not be part of this paragraph, so that it is now left to be tendered when the bill is gone through.

Thursday [January] 19[14]

WE spent the whole day entirely upon a dispute whether or no we should send out a writ for the election of a new knight of the shire for the county of Devon. The case is this: Christopher, now Duke of Albemarle, in the life of his father was chosen knight of the shire of Devon, and sat among us. His father being now dead at 12 months since, he has ever since and does still forbear to sit with us, as being now a peer of the kingdom; but he is not indeed called up to the House of Lords to sit with them because he is now but 19 years old, and none can sit in that House till he is 21; and whether his place in our House be void before he have right to sit in the Upper House is the sole question.

Much was said that it is unreasonable that he should lose

14. See above, p. 51 n.

his place with us before that he have right to sit in the Lords'
House:

1. And so having a double capacity that seems to entitle
him to both places, he should now be judged incapable of
sitting in either.

2. That we can not take notice of his father being dead
before the Lords require their member from us.

3. That he is not a peer till he has voted in parliament
among the peers.

4. That my Lord's father and the Earl of Sandwich sat
with us.

But it seemed to me that nothing can be more clear than
that his place is void, and the writ for electing another knight
should issue.

1. For as he has forborn hitherto coming to us by a year's
space, so it is certain he never will come to us, and if he
should the Lords would punish him for so doing.

2. That if he should sit with us, or break any order of the
House, or should be absent when the House is called, we could
not send him to the Tower or punish him pecuniarily as we
do our own members, for the Lords would oppose us.

3. If he should be invaded in his privilege he could not
come to us to do him right, but must go to the Lords.

4. In this bill of subsidy it is plain he must be taxed with
the Lords, and not among the Commons.

5. If he should commit any crime he must certainly be
tried by the peers, and not by a jury of commoners.

All this makes it plain that he is already a peer, though
he [does] not sit in their House by a particular constitution
of that House grounded, I conceive, upon this reason; that*
that House being a court of judicature, no one that is under
age can have a voice there, as none under 21 years can be
made a judge in Westminster Hall, they being not before
that time of years of discretion in the eyes of the law;
whereas the House of Commons, being no court of judicature,

---

* *That that House . . . in Westminster Hall* underscored in MS.

persons under age have been frequently admitted into it. (By the way, it was said by several persons that no man under age ought to sit in our House, and I think my Lord Coke is somewhere of that opinion,[15] but I am sure the constant practice of that House has been otherwise; and none did name any precedent where anyone has been turned out for being under age.)

As for the arguments on the other side:

1. It is very frequent that persons should be in no capacity to sit in either House, and it is the case of the Duke of Somerset, the Earl of Huntingdon, and divers others at this time, who being peers, and being under age can not sit in either House, for their minority excludes them from the Upper House, and for our House it is certain no peer can represent or be represented by the Commons of England.

2. And the death of the father is so notorious as we cannot but take notice of it, and if any one member do inform the House of the death of another member, the House never refuses to take notice of it, but sends out a writ immediately.

3. And that he can not be a peer till he do sit in parliament is a great mistake for the reasons before given; and some are peers all their lives which never yet can sit at all in parliament, as women that are baronesses by inheritance, as the Lady Dispenser was and the Lady Ruthen now is.

4. And the old Duke of Albemarle and the Earl of Sandwich did sit indeed in the Convention some days after they were peers, but it was, as I conceive, after they had their warrants for their honors, but not after the great seals were passed; or if they did it passed *sub silentium;* we thought ourselves much honored by the company of two blue ribbons, and would not call upon them to remove till they fairly told us of it themselves and took leave of us.

For these reasons the House did think fit to send out a writ for the choosing a new knight in the place of the Duke of Albemarle, who by the honor descended on him by the death of his father is removed from us, it being indeed very

15. Coke, *The Fourth Part of the Institutes* (1797), p. 46.

unreasonable that the county of Devon should want their representative in parliament.

Memo: During this debate there arose another which took up a very great deal of time. SIR JOHN NORTHCOT had moved that we should put off this debate, it being not certain to us that the place was void, or that my Lord Albemarle would not come again and claim it.

MR. SAMUEL ROLLES answered he wondered that gentleman would think it too soon to send out a writ for the election, when he himself had sent out warrants already to dispose the freeholders to the election of one Mr. Fortescue.

SIR JOHN NORTHCOT replied it was not so, and the other answered he had them there in his hand, and desired they might be read.

And long it was debated whether these words "it is not so" were offensive and unparliamentary, but that was laid aside as being a usual phrase, and no more than one man's affirmation and the other's negation.

Then whether those papers should be read, nobody affirming they were original, but at last by consent of SIR JOHN NORTHCOT they were read.

There were 5 of them in all, 4 of them to the same purpose; viz., a letter of the lord lieutenant, the Earl of Bath, to the deputy lieutenants, recommending to them the election of Mr. Fortescue as a loyal, worthy, understanding, and public-spirited man. These letters the deputy lieutenants, of which 2 were of our House—Sir John Northcot and Sir Courteney Poole—sent to the high constables to be communicated to the freeholders, with some recommendations of the thing; the 5th was also to the same purpose, but* added that the constables should return to him the names of all such as were willing to give their voices for Mr. Fortescue, but this was not subscribed by any of our members, but by one Woollycomb, or such a name.

The House all along spoke with great respect of the Earl

* *But added . . . for Mr. Fortescue* underscored in MS.

of Bath, and would not suffer anything done to reflect in any
measure upon him; as to our members, they called very ear-
nestly to have them withdraw, but they were not ordered to
do so; neither do I think it regular they should do so. Indeed,* when the House have agreed of the fact, and voted
that a misdemeanor, I think they may then be commanded to
withdraw while the House considers the punishment, but not
before. And, indeed, all they had done did not deserve any
great reproof for ought I saw. But at last, waiving all this
particular fact, (which if there be anything irregular in it,
will most properly come in at the hearing of the case before
the committee of privilege) they went upon a more general
consideration of this way of prepossessing the minds of the
electors, and in a manner awing them, and came to this general vote: that all warrants, or letters in form of warrants, or
any letters whatsoever to the sheriffs, constables, or other
officers, to be communicated to the freeholders or other electors when a knight of a shire or other member of parliament
is to be elected, is unparliamentary, and a prejudice to the
freedom of elections.

Friday [January] 20[16]

THIS day at ten the House resolved into a grand committee,
and Mr. Seymour took the chair and proceeded in the bill of
supply. The paragraph we went upon was that of taxing all
personal estates, goods, merchandise, and stock in trade at 6s.
for every 100 pound.

First it was moved by Mr. Coleman that this would comprehend money again which had been taxed before, that being
still personal estate, and therefore the words "personal estate
not before rated by this act" should be added; which was
agreed unto.

Then as to the main question, Mr. Gould of Devonshire

* *Indeed, when the House . . . but not before* underscored in MS.
16. Grey's report of this debate is much fuller.

made a long and studied speech against the whole paragraph, dilating much upon the nature of manufactures, the advance of human industry, and the inconvenience of scanting men's shops; after which we entered into a long debate which at last ended in this, that there should be an exception out of this clause for all stock upon land, and for all the product of land in the hands of the occupier of the land, or first owner; the meaning being that corn in the barn, or wool in the chamber, flax, hemp, hops, and such like not yet sold should not be taxed.

Saturday [January] 21[17]

WE resolved again into a grand committee upon the subsidy bill.

The first paragraph was concerning the taxing of offices, which stand in the bill at 2s. per pound; and it was carried that there should be an abatement of a 3rd part in consideration of the charges they were at in the execution thereof. And I did concur therein, though upon the division of the House most of the court party went against it, because indeed it seemed to me unreasonable at the first, that offices, which at most owe but for life, and 3 parts of 4 of them are but during his Majesty's pleasure, should pay double to estates of an inheritance.

Then it was moved by Colonel Birch that the word "promotions" should come in and be added, because that would bring in all the dignified clergy, but that was rejected.

Then we came to the next paragraph, which was whether the subsidy should be at 12d. or 8d. the pound, and this held us till 3 of the clock, and then the question was put in these terms: whether in this paragraph should be added a clause in these words, "a 3rd part of the said estate being deducted for the support of the family," and the committee being divided, the ayes were 114, and the noes were 124.

17. Dering's report of this day's activity is better than Grey's.

I were in the negative:

1. Because I thought we had no power to do it, the House having expressly tied us up to raising a sum near 800,000, which by this means could not possibly be done, for we have abated upon money, upon stock, and upon offices, and if we abate here it is not possible it should hold out in any measure.

2. I did not hear anybody offer to maintain that this 8*d.* would raise the intended sum, and I were clear of opinion for my own part that it would not.

3. That the argument that the fleet could not now be out 8 months was not considerable, since this money was not given for setting out the fleet, but for his Majesty's occasions in general, and for support of the government.

The reasons why I conceive that this money will not hold out to raise the intended sum are these:

1. Our vote is to raise a sum of money for present supply of his Majesty's occasions, near and not exceeding 800,000; which in common understanding and acceptation of the words must be at least 750,000.

2. The tax upon money, supposing that we shall find 4 millions of money at interest which undoubtedly we never shall, will yet at 10*s.* per cent amount to but 20,000. The stock in trade, if we do find 20 millions taxable above debts, which we never shall, yet at 6*s.* per cent amount to 60,000. The offices cannot possibly amount unto 20,000. So there remains to be raised upon land to make up 750,000, the sum of 650,000.

Now I take the whole revenue of England at present not to exceed 12 millions a year, which at 12*d.* per pound produces but 600,000, so there is deficient 50,000.

That the present yearly value of England is not above 12 millions, I deduce from these estimates:

1. A tax of 70,000 per mensem which raised 840,000 pounds in a year did require 2*s.* in the pound, and consequently 12*d.* in the pound will produce but 420,000; but it being true that though the eastern and southern parts paid

2s., the north, and Cheshire, and Lancashire, and Wales paid but *12d.* and many under. I do therefore allow these at a medium, that *12d.* per pound, one with another, would have produced 600,000.

2. The content of England and Wales, being about 300 miles long and 200 broad, reduced into a square makes a square of 250 miles every way, which by geometrical computation contains about 50 million of English acres. Now I conceive that, take one with another of all manner of sorts, 4–6 per acre is a good rate, and that comes to six millions per annum.

3. Again, cast out one 4th part or something more for all highways, commons, bogs, barren mountains, and such like unprofitable land, and I do conceive there will not then remain above 36 millions of profitable acres,[18] and that a noble per acre throughout is very sufficient valuation, which does amount to twelve millions per annum.

4. That there is yet another way of estimate, which is by what is bid and offered for a commodity, it being a rule of everything that *tanti est quanti vendi potest,* it is so much worth as by persons versed and trading in that manner will be given for it; that we had heard upon other occasions in this House for the customs for the new excise upon foreign commodities, [and] for the additional duty upon ale and beer, we had undertaken [to be] ready to make good the sums we had estimated them at, but nobody at all had yet ventured to undertake this at the same rate; if they would, though I had no power to make the bargain, yet I could easily say that I thought they would do the King very acceptable service, and such as I dare well join with them in.

5. After all, it was unavoidable that the King could not receive the whole of what should be given him by the act, but

18. Dering overestimates. There are altogether less than thirty-eight million acres in England and Wales. At the end of the 17th century, Gregory King estimated that there were twenty-seven million profitable acres. (H. C. Darby, ed., *Historical Geography of England before 1860,* p. 394.)

in things left to so much uncertainty, and to be raised in so many particulars, must lose at least a tenth; that as to the argument that now we need not give so much because the time of the year was now spent or would be before this act passed, and so we could not have our ships out so long as was pretended, I thought that was not to be urged, since these very gentlemen that now used [it] had before declared that they did not give this money for setting out the fleet, but because his Majesty asked it, and that he might use it as he thought fit for the support of the government; in sum, that I did not conceive we had still the same necessities upon us that we had; I were sure we had the same affections and inclinations to his Majesty's service that we had when we voted this sum, and therefore prayed it might be expressed in the same words, and the same sum stand as it now does in the paragraph.

Monday [January] 23[19]

THE debate of the House was wholly taken up upon these words, "Mines of coal, tin, and lead," whether they should stand in the bill; and very many did speak for leaving them out; viz., Sir Robert Howard, Mr. Boscawen, Mr. Spry, Colonel Sandys, Mr. Buller, Mr. Clarke, Sir Winston Churchill, and many others.

The arguments used for excusing them were these:

1. The uncertainty of the value.

2. That they never yet were charged in any act.

3. That the King had already a great duty from them, near a 6th part.

4. That there were many poor people concerned therein, which were the day workers and laborers in the mines.

5. That many persons had lost great estates by embarking in the mines.

6. That many laid out 3 or 4,000 pounds, and in 3 or 4 years should see no return.

19. Dering's and Grey's reports of this day's activities are similar.

7. That it was a commodity which was carried abroad to great profit of the nation, and therefore ought not to be charged for discouraging the trade.

8. That the owners of mines would rather lay down their works this year than pay the duty.

Those who spoke to keep them in were: the Attorney General, Colonel Birch, Sir Robert Atkins, Mr. Whorwood, myself. That which I said was chiefly to answer the objections:

1. That the uncertainty thereof was not greater than in merchandise and in many other trades which yet by the bill were to be taxed.

2. That if they had never been taxed, more reason to tax them now, and even to tax them higher than others, for money had never been taxed till now, and is therefore by this bill taxed double to land, and yet they were taxable before by the name of hereditaments, and by express name are ratable to the poor.

3. That the King had a 6th part of the value by way of duty was not sufficient to excuse them, for he had a far greater duty upon barley; viz., 50l. per cent, for the duty of old and new excise; viz., 4–9 per barrel on strong beer, will come to 8s. the quarter upon barley, which is one half of the full value of the barley, and yet we tax it by this bill.

4. The day workers would not be concerned at all, nothing going to be laid upon their labor; and as for the owners, nothing was intended to be charged but what the mine could be reasonably valued at as a yearly profit over and above all charges.

5. If many had lost by ill accidents as fire and water, I could name many others who had gained very much and constantly by them, and I need not go far for instances. (In truth, several members of the House were pregnant proofs of it, my Lord St. John alone having at least 5,000 pounds per annum by his lead mines, but I did not name him.)

6. If many laid out money 3 or 4 years before they saw their return of it, they did not lose by their account at last,

and was as good profit as buying a reversion which comes in with treble advantage at last.

7. If tin and lead were commodities we did export, and therefore ought not to be charged, I could not allow that reason, since cloth is a commodity ten times more considerable than that, which yet the wisdom of the House did think fit to charge in this very bill.

8. To say the owners would lay down their workers for this year while the tax lasts, and then set them up again is to say they had rather lose 19 parts than pay the King one, the duty imposed being but one shilling in the pound of the clear yearly value; and I thought there was none of the owners of the mines would take that expedient to save themselves the duty, and therefore desired the words might stand as they now are.

It was then moved that the questions might be put severally for coal, tin, and lead, there being some reasons for one which were not for the other. And this, being regular, was done, and upon the several questions, all carried in the affirmative that the words "coal, tin, and lead" should stand in.

Then the question was put for alum mines, and carried presently in the affirmative.

Then the question [was] moved for iron works, at which Sir Robert Carr* moved that it is not in the power of the committee to add any particulars to the supply which the House had not referred to us. And I think he was in the right, only the committee may agree if they think fit to move the House that any particular may be added. However, iron works were put to the question, and carried in the negative.

Tuesday [January] 24²⁰

I WENT to the House but stayed not above an hour, being taken with a fit of an ague, as I had been on Sunday before.

* *Sir Robert Carr . . . referred to us* underscored in MS.
20. Grey reports but one speech, and that refers to the subsidy bill.

The House did not enter, I think, upon the King's bill, being taken up with several private bills and motions, and particularly upon a breach of privilege committed upon a servant of Mr. John Howe, a member of the House. The bailiff complained of has applied himself to the House, and insisted that the person arrested is not Mr. Howe's servant, but* Mr. Howe averring that he is his menial servant, the House always gives that credit to a member in what he avers upon his own knowledge that they will hear no proof against it.

Wednesday [January] 25[21]

THE House went upon the amendments of the House of Lords made to the bill for Sir John Coventry, and disagreed to them all, and thereupon prayed a conference with the Lords.

Memo: It being questioned in the House, it was agreed that upon reading any amendments from the Lords to our bills, the proper question is with us whether agree or not agree to the amendments; if we do not agree then we are to desire a conference and to open to their lordships our reasons why we cannot agree to their amendments; then if the Lords do not yield to our reasons they are to desire a conference with us (a free conference, I think it is) to show us their reasons, and to maintain their amendments; and after that the proper question is whether we will adhere to our former votes or not adhere; and† if we adhere after a free conference we can not then go back, and if the Lords adhere also then the bill is lost. Yet I have known sometimes a reconference desired and granted, but I do not remember whether we had voted to adhere first or not. It‡ was said also, that when we have named one day and the Lords have named another day, then we can not name a third day but we must either stand to our

* *But Mr. Howe . . . proof against it* underscored in MS.
† *And if we adhere . . . bill is lost* underscored in MS.
‡ In the MS. a line is drawn down the margin from *It was said* to *part of the same amendment.*
21. Grey's account of this day's debates is similar to Dering's.

own or yield to theirs, but they may, if they see cause, amend their own amendments.

It was said to this by Sir Thomas Lee that [it] did not always hold, for where the amendment was only the alteration of a day, which was but as one word for another, we must take our own or take the Lords' day, but where the amendment was of several periods we might retain some part of their amendment and then assent to the other with an addition of our own. And certain it is, we may agree to one part of an amendment, and yet reject another part of the same amendment.

Thursday January 26[22]

I went not to the House for fear of my ague, of which I had had two fits the Sunday and Tuesday before, but I thank God it came not.

Friday [January] 27[23]

I were at the House; some progress in the King's bill but nothing memorable, only the great debate was whether the assessors for this royal subsidy should be upon oath. The reasons against it were:

1. The multiplication of oaths throughout the land.

2. The great and evident danger of perjuries.

3. That customary oaths were very little regarded, witness the oaths of church wardens and constables.

4. That a penalty of twenty pounds will do better and prevail more with them.

5. That we shall deter all gentlemen from acting, if it be upon oath.

6. That it is new, and not practised before.

22. Omitted in Grey also.
23. Grey's report of this day's activity is similar to Dering's.

It was answered: that oaths were necessary and usual in all places of Christendom; that nobody had more for any security nor could there be greater; that the age was not so deplorable but we could not find 4 or 5 men in a hundred to make assessors who would reverence an oath; that otherwise this would be the most arbitrary proceeding in the world, and I cannot be sued for an acre of land nor a twopenny trespass, but I must have witnesses upon oath, and must have a jury also upon oath, than much more here; that a penalty of 20 pounds may indeed be more considerable in the country than any sum that can be saved in the return of any man's farm or demesnes, but that could signify little in the town here, where personal estates of ten, twenty, forty thousand pound were to be taxed who might well pay the assessors their fines of twenty pounds to be spared; that we shall not deter but encourage gentlemen to act, since they will now have a rule to guide them, that is, the oaths of the assessors, and the assessors themselves will have an answer to repress any man's importunity for favor, since they be under the strict obligation of an oath; and lastly that this is not new and unpractised, for in Queen Mary's time or Edward VI's, it was so in the subsidy bill, and in Henry VI's not only the assessors were upon oath, but the commissioners had power to examine the party himself upon his own oath. If this had been omitted in the late acts for monthly assessments it was not to be wondered at because the whole proportion being set up by the act upon the counties, they were concerned among themselves to see that none did escape, for if they did the neighborhood must make it up.

Upon the question the assessors' oaths were kept in.

Saturday [January] 28[24]

We made a great progress in the King's bill; the matters being chiefly about the times of payment, the manner of col-

24. Omitted in Grey.

lecting, the allowances to the sub-collectors and high collectors. At last it was started whether the commissioners should
be responsible for the high collector, and some thought they
were, others thought they were not; the major part seemed
to believe that they were, since they are bound to take good
security of him; yet none thought this to be reasonable. It
was therefore propounded to make it clear, and to say plainly
they should not be responsible for him; but that looking a
little harsh it was proposed to leave out high collectors altogether, as needless, and the sub-collectors might pay it to the
receiver general; but the business of high collectors being in
many paragraphs which we had already passed, and could not
now recall, it was taken up at last as an expedient that the
head collectors should stand, but should be no other but depu-
ties to the receiver general, and appointed by him, and he be
responsible to the king for them; and also for his encouragement should have the fee and salary formerly allowed to the
high collector, which would be sure to recompense his pains.
And so it passed with this addition, that he should compel
no sub-collector to travel above ten miles.

Tuesday January 31[25]

SOME progress in the subsidy bill; most of the particulars,
being clauses of form and usual in other acts, were agreed,
the blanks for the times of assessment and payment filled up.

We called over the House again according to order, and
many were absent. The House upon debate did resolve to put
in the names of the absent members into the bill of subsidy
now before them, that they may both pay double subsidies,
and may also be known to their countries for neglectors of
their trust and duty.[26]

25. Grey reports only two speeches, and those are on the bill for settling
a bank and registry for deeds.
26. See below, p. 90.

Wednesday [February] 1[1]

WE proceeded in the King's bill and finished it, only there remained three clauses which had been postponed. One was about transferring of debts from other securities of the King's revenue upon this act; the clause now was too general, for the debate of the House was only to give leave to transfer such debts as are upon the customs, excise, and hearth money, not any upon the wine licenses or fee farms, and now the words of restriction as to these branches were not in, and therefore I moved such restrictive words might be added; which was thought reasonable.

In the afternoon I were at the committee of grievances, where the matter before us was concerning certain lighthouses erected in Ireland by the Earl of Arran (and Mr. Reading) by virtue of his Majesty's letters patent 16 July, 19th of his reign, for the maintaining whereof they demanded, and by the letters patent are empowered so to do, one penny per ton outwards and inwards of every vessel in Ireland, and ten shillings per annum of every fisher boat fishing upon that coast.

The counsels on both sides were very long, and they having done, it being now 8 of the clock, it was moved to adjourn the debate till the next sitting of the committee, and the committee being divided upon it, there were 36 for continuing the debate, and 32 for adjourning it. I were for the adjourning it, but the negative being carried, 26 or 27 of them who were for the adjourning it went away immediately with intention that all we being gone, the number remaining not being forty, there would be no committee and so there could be nothing done. I did not much like that expedient because it looked like a trick, an artifice to prevent things from coming to a fair debate at a time when all parties are ready and expect it, therefore I did sit it out, so that the whole number of the com-

1. Omitted in Grey.

mittee was 41, for* forty at least is necessary to every grand committee, as eight are said to be [to] a private committee, if a lesser quorum be not appointed by the House.

At nine they came to a vote, and voted that the collecting of one penny per ton upon his Majesty's English subjects by virtue of letters patent for the maintaining of certain light-houses in Ireland is a grievance.

Memo: This which I have entered concerning the light-houses was not on Wednesday but on Friday, the 3rd of February, for on Wednesday the first I attended his Majesty in council where was heard the complaint and address of Colonel Richard Talbot in behalf of the Irish Catholics in Ireland who are not restored to their land there. The substance of the complaint was to magnify the King's declaration and to arraign the acts of settlement and explanation, and was managed by Serjeant Scroggs, Mr. Aylaph, and Mr. Offley. On the other side was only the attorney general, who gave a very large and full account in what the acts did vary from the declaration, and by what authority they did so, and for what reasons; and that in general they were not more advantageous to the English than the declaration itself was. The business held very late, and the King† at last declared that he would not vary from the acts of settlement and explanation which could not be allowed without shaking the whole settlement of that kingdom, nor could indeed be changed in any clause or particular without another act of parliament, and should that be had, in Ireland it could never pass, for there the adventurers, soldiers, and others concerned against it would always be for the majority of the Lower House, (and so they would be in the Lords' House, and in the very council table) and in England it would be very doubtful whether it would pass, and as doubtful whether it be advisable to subject that kingdom so absolutely to the parliament of England. Therefore his Majesty resolved to leave the settlement as it is entire;

* *For forty . . . appointed by the House* underscored in MS.
† *The King . . . another act of parliament* underscored in MS.

and if any undisposed lands be found out or other way can be proposed for their relief, which did not at all affect the settlement, the King would be willing to apply it to the relief of these petitioners.

Memo: We, the commissioners of Ireland, were summoned to appear, but there being nothing said by the complainants against the execution of the acts, but altogether against the acts themselves, we held ourselves unconcerned and were therefore only hearers, without objecting or answering anything at all.

[Thursday February] 2

THURSDAY being Candlemas Day we did not sit.

Friday [February] 3²

WE proceeded upon the bill of subsidy, and agreed the clause for debtors deducting from their creditors, which is voted shall be at six shillings the hundred pound for every hundred pound owing for money at interest.

Saturday [February] 4³

WE proceeded on the matter reported us from the conference the Lords had desired, and some particular amendments offered by them we did agree unto. Some others of ours they had agreed unto, but the first and the last we did not agree in, and therefore resolved to desire a free conference with them upon these things, it being regular to do so.

It was also said that we, having named one day in the bill, cannot now name another day, though we find our day of the 16th of February is too short, but the Lords may do it.

It was said also that we may disagree to their amendments,

---

2. Omitted in Grey.
3. Grey's report is much fuller than Dering's.

and that we may also vote ourselves* unsatisfied with their reasons, and none of this be conclusive to us till we do vote to adhere to what we have done.

Monday [February] 6⁴

SIR ROBERT HOLT informed the House that lately in the parish next to him in Warwickshire during the time of divine service five men armed with swords and pistols came into the church and took away by force a gentleman out of the church, and carried him to prison, one of them being a bailiff arresting him; and therefore prayed that a bill might be brought in to the House to prevent all abuses, but especially arrests on the Sabbath day.

SIR EDMUND WYNDHAM added yet a more horrible impiety of one taken away lately by the bailiffs not only out of the church, but at the very time of the sacrament, while he was upon his knees at that holy duty, and had already received the bread, they hurried him away, not suffering him to receive the holy cup.

The House were moved with just indignation at these abominations, and voted that a bill be brought in to prevent such abuses for the time to come; for men that had done it, it did not appear how we should reach them.

Upon this MR. CROUCH moved that the increase of papists in England was very notorious, and the complaint against it was very high, and that it would become the wisdom of this House to take some care to prevent the further growth of it.

This was seconded by SIR THOMAS DOLEMAN, and thirded by SIR TREVOR WILLIAMS who informed the House that half the county of Monmouth was already papists, and many of them turned of late, and that he verily thought there was more popish priests in that county than Protestant ministers.

---

* *Ourselves unsatisfied . . . we have done* underscored in MS.

4. Grey begins his report where Dering leaves off, and gives an account of the conference with the Lords.

This took very well in the House and was ordered accordingly.

It was added by MR. GARRAWAY that we should consider of the Jews also, who had two synagogues in London; to inquire by what authority they came there, and how they behaved themselves.[5]

SIR RICHARD FORD, at this present lord mayor of London, made the same motion, and so these matters are all recommended to the same committee.

Then we turned the House into a grand committee to consider of the bill of registers, and Sir Robert Carr took the chair.

It was first moved by Sir Solomon Swale that every manor should be in the nature of a copyhold manor, and no part of that manor should be encumbered or alienated but by entry in the court rolls.

1. But this could not be because then you must keep courts every 3 weeks or month, which would cost more than it was worth to the lords of manors.

2. Many lands were doubtful of what lords they held.

3. What should become when the manors themselves were encumbered or mortgaged by the lords thereof?

Mr. Dowdeswell moved that instead of entering of judgments as they now do in the courts of Westminster, which is extremely chargeable to search for, and difficult to find, all judgments, statutes, and recognizances might be entered in the country where the lands do lie.

Sir Richard Temple moved that there might be an office of enrollments, and that it was enough to oblige every man to enter his deed there, and have it subscribed by the master of the office.

That which comes nearest to the sense of the House seemed to be this: that there should be an office of enrollment not in

5. The investigation of the Jews was apparently not carried out. (H. S. Q. Henriques, *The Jews and the English Law*, pp. 148–9.)

London, but in every county one; that all judgments, statutes, recognizances, mortgages, leases, deeds of rent charges, etc., which affect the lands may be here entered and subscribed by the master of the office; that no more should be entered in the office but the names of the parties and date of deeds with some short description of the place where the lands affected do lie; that nobody shall be bound by this to enter any deeds in this office but that he please, but none shall be good against a purchaser but that which is enrolled; that there should be very little or no retrospect; that no deed shall be made good or made void by this enrollment otherwise than it would be by law; that by no means there should be any enrollment or entering of deeds at large as the most pernicious and destructive thing that may be.

But before we came to any resolution we were informed that the Lords were come to the Painted Chamber in order to the free conference we had desired, so this debate was at an end for the present.

Tuesday [February] 7[6]

A LONG bill read for settling the estate of the young Earl of Shrewsbury and buying out the jointure of the Countess his mother. This came down from the Lords and was read now the first time.

Then SIR JOHN BRAMSTON tendered a bill for enabling the bishops in their several dioceses to dispose of the personal estates of intestates.

This was opposed at first, but afterwards it was acknowledged to be very necessary, since for want of it many the times the wife (or other administrator) went away with the whole personal estate, and all the children were undone; and though the bishops did usually take bonds of them when they committed the administration, yet it signified nothing, for those bonds were always judged void by the judges in West-

6. Omitted in Grey.

minster Hall. Yet they would not receive this bill, because in a matter of so great importance, it was not fit any member should of his own head bring it in, but ought first to move the House, and then if they approved it, they would order a bill to be brought in for that purpose. And so it was ordered in this case.

Then we turned into a grand committee to proceed in the King's supply. The clause debated was for transferring the King's debts from other branches of his revenue upon this subsidy bill; and whether the bankers should have it in their choice to transfer their debts upon it or whether the creditors of the bankers should transfer their debts (and some the bankers to place them upon this bill, and the bankers to discharge the King of so much as is transferred) was the question.

For the first were Sir Thomas Clifford, Sir John Duncombe, Sir Thomas Osborne, Sir Thomas Littleton, Sir George Downing, and Colonel Birch, and Sir William Backwell.

For the second were Sir Thomas Lee, Sir Thomas Meres, Mr. Garraway, Mr. Whorwood, Sir John Knight, etc.

I were against both, and against all transferring upon this bill, which would be quite swallowed up by it, and turn to a private satisfaction of the worst part of his Majesty's debts, for the best would not transfer themselves. And the first was extremely inconvenient to the King; the second unjust and unpracticable.

But the question being put for the creditors to enforce the bankers to transfer them upon the act, the yeas were 82, the negatives 64.

Wednesday [February] 8[7]

WE proceeded not in the bill for the supply, for the whole day was taken up upon a report from the committee of griev-

7. Grey's report is similar to Dering's.

ances concerning the lighthouses erected in Ireland, and for which a penny per ton was demanded by Mr. Reading the patentee, (though the patent be made in the Earl of Arran's name), and after a very long debate the House resolved to leave out the word "illegal" brought in by the committee of grievances, and only voted it a common grievance, pursuing therein the words of a former vote in the case of a lighthouse at Milfordhaven pretended to by Mr. Brouncker.

Memo: In this case they did not put the regular question "agree or not agree with the committee," but came to a question which seemed more to reconcile the sense of the House.

Memo: The lighthouses are at Dublin, Carrickfergus, Waterford, and Kinsale. That complained of is at Dublin on the head of Howth, which is, I think, useful to those who come on that coast at night, and the testimonies given against the usefulness of it were very inconsiderable, but the thing passed currently in the House, while some were afraid it should be voted illegal, and so have further intrenched upon the prerogative, and others were glad to damn it in any form lest there should be a color thereby for the King to raise any money in any kind without act of parliament.

I spoke only as to the usefulness of it in that place, not to the power of the King to raise money for the maintaining it.

Thursday [February] 9[8]

WE proceeded upon a bill of indigent officers, and referred it to a committee to examine the accounts of monies received, and money in arrears, but withdrew the power in the bill given for reassessment.

Then we proceeded on the bill for the King's supply, and perfected the clause for transferring upon the bill of subsidy, which I were against.

8. Grey gives a full account of the conference with the Lords.

Friday February 10[9]

We proceeded upon the bill for subsidy, and particularly upon a clause concerning the bankers, [in] which [it] was voted they should pay 15*s*. per centum for all the money they had lent the King, and should deduct 10*s*. of it from their creditors.

Then the question was put whether in order to [do] it the commissioners should have power to send for and inspect their books, and the committee dividing upon it, it was carried in the negative, the affirmatives being 67, and the negatives 94.

There was also a report concerning the manner of election at Seaforth in Sussex, which the committee of privileges had reported to be in the populace and not in the select burgesses, and upon the question, the House dividing, it was carried in agreement with the committee.

Memo: Mr. Gratwick and Mr. Morley, 2 of the 3 pretenders died during the contest.

Saturday [February] 11[10]

We proceeded upon a free conference with the Lords concerning Sir John Coventry's bill, and the chief difference was about a clause giving some particular privilege to parliament men for the future, in case of malicious wounding or maiming. And* we had the day before voted ourselves unsatisfied with their lordships reasons for rejecting that clause, and now we inclined to submit to them, and agree to cast it out. The question was how to do it; to go from our former votes without hearing any further reasons was absurd. The Speaker proposed that we might enter it under the same vote of yes-

---

* In the MS. a line is drawn down the margin of the whole page from *and we had* to *instructed their committee accordingly for the conference.*
9. Omitted in Grey.   10. Omitted in Grey.

terday, that we were dissatisfied with their lordships' reasons, yet rather than retard the bill we would comply with them. This was indeed very well if it had been done the same day, but since that day was passed, now to enter a vote of this day as if it had been voted yesterday I could not for my part consent to, for it is not truth, and besides, the consequences of it might be dangerous.

At last SIR THOMAS LITTLETON moved that we might declare ourselves dissatisfied with their Lordships' reasons, but we would comply with them therein, and for the clause they had refused, we would bring in a bill on purpose for it, and this seemed the most plausible and honorable retreat we could think of, and so the House resolved upon it, and instructed their committee accordingly for the conference.

Monday [February] 13[11]

WE proceeded to finish the bill for supply by a royal subsidy, and the last clause was for paying double by such parliament men as had been found absent without such excuse as had been allowed by the House. The committee divided upon the question whether this clause should be added to the bill or not, and the affirmatives were 68, and the negatives were 61.

Then we proceeded to the preamble, which was all that remained of this bill, and there it was moved by Sir John Cotton* that in the preamble it would be expressed that this money was given to maintain† the triple league between England, Holland, and Sweden.

But it was moved by Mr. Garraway that we should not meddle with those matters of state which were not submitted to us nor of which we were not all informed, and besides we should be wary of interesting ourselves in those leagues, lest we should be called upon to maintain them; and put us in

---

* *Sir John Cotton* underscored in MS.
† *Maintain . . . Holland, and Sweden* underscored in MS.
11. Omitted in Grey.

mind of our former votes to stand by his Majesty with our
lives and fortunes in the war with the Dutch, and how that
had been laid back upon us to oblige us to very great sums of
money, and therefore we had better give it absolutely to his
Majesty for his supplies* and for discharge of his debts
without inquiring what he would do with it, or how they were
contracted.

Tuesday [February] 14[12]

WE proceeded according to former order to call over the
House first, and then to call again the defaulters in order to
put them into a clause in the act for paying double subsidies.
The defaulters were many but the greatest part of them
excused. I believe about thirty stood unexcused. Upon one
the House divided whether he would be excused or not. The
yeas who went out were 185, and the noes that stayed in were
86. I were in the negative as to the gentleman who was Colonel Williams, (alias Cromwell) because he had particularly
asked leave of the House to go down, and was expressly denied it, so that there was much less reason to excuse him than
any other whatsoever.

After this one we entered upon the report of the amendments made by the committee to the bill of subsidy, and MR.
SEYMOUR, the chairman, reported them to the House, but it
being late the House adjourned the debate of them till tomorrow morning.

Wednesday [February] 15[13]

WE proceeded in the report of the amendments to the bill of
subsidy. The great debate was upon 3 questions:
   1. Whether the bankers should pay 15s. every hundred

---

* *His supplies . . . they were contracted* underscored in MS.
12. Omitted in Grey.   13. Omitted in Grey.

pounds they had lent his Majesty; which was carried in the affirmative.

2. Then whether the bankers should deduct from their creditors 10*s*. for every hundred pounds, and so bear only the 5*s*. themselves. This was much opposed because when gentlemen did lend their money to the bankers it was as lawful to lend it to them as to any other persons and still is, and why then should they be punished for so doing? And again the bankers have lent at ten per cent to the King, which is the reason why we do differentiate them from other men, but they who have lent the bankers have only taken lawful interest, yes, many of them under six per cent, and therefore [there is] no reason to tax them at an extraordinary rate. But these were both carried in the affirmative.

The third question was upon the clause of transferring, which was long debated, and at last it was thrown out. I were the first that moved against it, it being evident to me that it would devour 3 parts of the benefit of this bill, and not certain, no not probable that it would free any one branch of his Majesty's revenue, which was the most plausible reason to introduce it. That as there was no service to the King in it, so there was no satisfaction to the people, and all the advantage of it redounded to certain persons who had no reason to expect it from us, nor had so much as petitioned us for it. And other reasons: as that it was inconsistent with our votes, which were for a present supply to his Majesty in the bill, which if we did transfer the old debts upon it, it would not yield one penny; that it was an uncertain fund and therefore could not bear any great weight if men should be enabled to transfer upon it, since they would be jealous of coming anything near the outside of the security; that it would discredit the bill, and discourage the commissioner and assessors if all the money should be known to be disposed of before the bill was put in execution; that in sum it did transfer in the whole nature of the bill, and from a present supply to his Majesty which the King had desired and we intended, turns it into a

mere collateral security for the bankers and their creditors.
And if any gentleman should yet think that this were reasonable to be done, it were certainly more reasonable to do it
upon the other bills which are yet behind and which are intended for payment of his Majesty's debts, than upon this,
which was desired by him and intended by us to be for a
present supply of ready money for his occasions. For these
and other reasons added by others, at last the House resolved
to cast out the clause for transferring.

Thursday [February] 16[14]

WE proceeded upon the report of the amendments to the bill
of supply; the chief debate was upon two points.

1. Whether the commissioners should be sworn, upon which
the House divided, and the yeas were 86, the noes were 185.

I were in the negative, finding so great a resolution in the
gentlemen generally not to act if they were sworn, so that
the King would be necessitated to employ strangers therein,
which would lose him more or cost him more than gentlemen
acting upon their honor and fidelity to him would do. Besides
the assessors are now upon oath, and therefore [it is] less
necessary to put the commissioners upon oath, the weight
lying chiefly upon the assessors. And thirdly, the King, having the nomination of the commissioners, may secure himself
the choice of such commissioners as he can trust, and if we
had nominated commissioners as we used to do, it had been
more reasonable to bind them by oath.

The second question was about a clause to make all defaulters pay double subsidy, to which end a clause should be put
in this bill. The House divided upon it, and the yeas were 98,
the noes were 115.

I were in the negative for these reasons:

1. Because this was to confess we had no power to punish
our own members without the help of the Lords.

14. Grey's report is almost the same as Dering's.

2. This was a new and yet unprecedented way.

3. It was too grievous to print all these persons and record them to all posterity for betrayers or at least neglectors of their trust.

4. We had other ways in our own power; as sending for them by the sergeant at their own charge, and then sending them to the Tower if they could show no good excuse.

5. We had not heard their excuses, and some gentlemen did affirm upon their own knowledge that many of them had just excuses.

6. I thought not fit to agree to a clause with a blank which did not yet appear to us that we could with justice fill up.

And this being over, we put the question for engrossing the bill; which was passed.

Friday [February] 17[15]

THIS day we received the report from the committee appointed to consider of the growth of popery. The report was made by SIR TREVOR WILLIAMS, who reported these following causes:

1. The great resort of Jesuits and popish priests into this kingdom more than ordinary, especially to London and Westminster.

2. Several chapels where mass was publicly celebrated, besides the houses of ambassadors.

3. Several fraternities and convents for popish priests, particularly one at St. James, besides the Queen's chapel, and one at Comb in Herefordshire.

4. Selling of popish catechisms and books.

5. General remissness in convicting.

6. Freedom of papists from chargeable offices, as sheriffs, deputy lieutenants.

7. Presentation of livings where advowsons belong to papists, who bestow them on scandalous men.

15. Omitted in Grey.

8. Sending children beyond sea for education.

9. No exchequer process against any men since the King's coming, or very few though many certified.

10. Peter Talbot Archbishop of Ireland, and so treated.

The remedies propounded were to petition the King to command by proclamation all Jesuits and priests to leave the Kingdom; that his Majesty do command the laws against papists to be put in execution; that all English people be restrained from hearing mass; that no office or employment, civil or military, be bestowed on papists; that notice be taken of all fraternities or convents of friars; that his Majesty be moved to send for Peter Talbot, the titular Archbishop of Dublin, and . . . Plunket, the titular Primate of Ireland.

Saturday [February] 18[16]

I WERE not there, being forced to keep my bed by a fit of the colic, the second that ever I had, the first being about 5 weeks since.

Monday [February] 20[17]

I WERE not there, not thinking it safe to adventure out so soon, finding myself very apt since my last sickness to take cold.

Tuesday [February] 21[18]

THE House proceeded upon the business of Lindsey Level, which took up the whole day; but only the address concerning the growth of popery was carried up to the Lords for their consent by Sir Trevor Williams.

16. Omitted in Grey.   17. Omitted in Grey.
18. Omitted in Grey.

Wednesday [February] 22[19]

A BILL brought in to advance the herring fishing was read the first time, and there being several things very unreasonable, the House inclined to throw it out, but upon debate they suffered it to be withdrawn, and ordered another bill to be brought in for that purpose.

Memo: This was the first bill that I remember withdrawn by a question, for two others this session which were withdrawn, were so by consent without a question, and that not by chance but upon advice, there being no precedent before of withdrawing a bill after the House were possessed of it, but the question usually is for reading a second time, which if it pass in the negative the bill is rejected; and the consequence of it may be great, for a bill that is once read and then withdrawn again, may be tendered again the second time the same session, which a bill that is read and rejected cannot be; and he that should tender it the second time in hope to pass that in a thin House which would not go down in a full House, would not break therein any order of the House, though he would perhaps hazard his discretion, or at least, any little variation would serve to warrant a second tender, whereas if the bill be rejected, nothing of that nature nor to that purpose ought to be tendered again the same session.

Then we went into a grand committee to consider of the bill for an additional excise upon ale and beer, and Mr. Seymour had the chair, and read over the whole bill, and ordered by the House to proceed upon the several paragraphs of it the next day.

Thursday [February] 23[20]

THE great debate was concerning several clauses in this bill for searching of private houses, which should be said to brew,

19. Grey reports the subsidy debate, but does not mention the procedural point.
20. Omitted in Grey.

and commanding all those which should brew, though for their own private use, in any corporation, or within 4 miles of any corporation (who had not formerly used to brew their own drinks) to be subject to the duty of excise. This was long argued pro and con, but it grew so high that I saw plainly if private houses were not excused, the whole bill would be cast out; and the thing being very reasonable in itself, and no color appearing why those gentlemen who live within 4 miles of a corporation should be under a prohibition of brewing their own beer if they pleased, especially in case a brewer should brew very bad or unwholesome drink, which might often fall out, I went down to the treasurer and to the attorney general to tell them my opinion was that we should leave out all that concerned private houses, or else the whole bill would be cast out; and they, being of the same mind also, Mr. Treasurer moved himself, which gave the House great satisfaction, and so the bill was committed.

But Mr. Jones of the city making a long and sharp speech against the whole body of the bill, even after this accommodation, then several things were urged, not now indeed for direct throwing out the bill but as previous instructions to the committee.

Memo: It is not very unusual to give such previous instructions to a grand committee of the whole House, because in the committee every man has freedom of debate, and to speak what and as often as he please, but it being insisted upon with great earnestness, it was admitted, and several things resolved about the conviction about altering the penalties and the like; some things were urged to be resolved in the House, which had been debated before the bill was committed, and the bill* being committed upon the debate of the House, the House could not resume them again before they had a report from the committee, as was well observed by Mr. Waller, and was yielded by the other side; but then they started new things not mentioned or debated before the commitment, and

* *The bill . . . report from the committee* underscored in MS.

these they did proceed upon, though for my part I thought it unnecessary, for when a bill* is committed upon a debate, yet a grand committee may proceed upon parts not debated.

Friday [February] 24

THE House did not sit, it being holiday and the feast of St. Matthew.

Saturday [February] 25[21]

THE House proceeded again upon the bill for ale and beer, and made good progress in it.

They resolved the penalties should be allowed.

They reduced the additional duty of 15d. upon strong beer and 6d. per barrel upon small unto 9d. upon strong and 3d. upon small.

And several repartees were between some members of the House and Sir Thomas Clifford and Sir John Duncombe, the first bidding the others look to the event, for they had liberty to set what excise they would desire, and if the King's revenue was not sufficiently augmented by it, it was their fault who did not know what was best; the others answering that they had complied in all the abatements that had been proposed and were ready yet to take the judgment of the House in any particular they could object against, but could not be answerable for the event, no more than others who were as much bound to offer their opinions and as much freedom in so doing as they had.

But that which bred the longest debate was concerning the taking away all the statutes now in force for any excise of ale and beer, and licensing the alehouse keepers to sell at what rate they could get or exact from any person poor or rich, neighbor or traveller; and this was at last carried, and

---

* *A bill . . . parts not debated* underscored in MS.
21. Omitted in Grey.

that by a very great majority of voices, to my wonder, I confess, who were utterly against it.

The arguments used for it were:

1. That we did limit no price upon French stuffs and silks, and therefore no reason to set any upon our own commodities.

2. That we could set no just price because the price of malt did fall and rise.

3. That suffering men to sell at what price they would, they would brew beer of greater strength, and consequently spend more of our malt.

None of which arguments did at all move me, the mischief being far greater than the pretended convenience.

Monday [February] 27[22]

MONDAY was spent upon the other amendments to the bill, and ordered it to be reported the next day.

Tuesday [February] 28[23]

THE House received the report from the committee, and agreed [to] all the amendments, and ordered it to be engrossed.

Wednesday [March] 1[1]

WE received the subsidy bill from the Lords with several amendments which, being most of them liberal and for the errors of the clerks, we did agree unto.

In the latter end the Lords added three provisos:

1. That this act should not be drawn into example for the future to the prejudice of the rights of the Lords spiritual or

22. Omitted in Grey.

23. Grey reports only a short debate on the case of Mr. Robert Thomas.

1. For this date Grey reports the debate on the sugar refiners' petition which actually occurred on March 4.

temporal, or universities, colleges, hospitals, or Cinque Ports. This was agreed to without any debate.

2. That this act should not prejudice any contract between landlords and tenants for the payment of taxes and assessments. This received great debate, and at last the House divided upon it, but the odds appearing manifest, they who were for not agreeing did yield it without telling.

3. That no dwelling house of any peer should be broken upon for non-payment of any sum payable by this act, but in [the] presence of one of the commissioners. This received a great debate, and at last the House divided upon it. The yeas that were for agreeing with the Lords were 71, the noes for disagreeing were 92.[2]

Memo:* In this case the yeas were to go out, and did so, because it is a new thing as to the House of the Commons, though it be in our own bill, and arises from the Lords, whereas when the question is for agreeing or disagreeing with any amendment of a committee of our own then the noes do go out.

Then we read over a bill to prevent the growth of popery brought in by Sir Trevor Williams.

Then we read over a bill for the better observation of the Lord's day.

Thursday [March] 2[3]

WE read over the bill for additional duty upon ale and beer the third time, and sent it up to the Lords by Mr. Seymour.[4]

Then we read over the bill against popery the second time and committed it.

Then SIR ROBERT HOLT moved us to come to a resolution concerning some doubts in the hearth bill, and particularly

---

* This whole paragraph underscored in MS.
2. The *Journal* (IX, 210) reports the noes at 91.
3. Omitted in Grey.
4. Actually this bill had its third reading the day before. (*C.J.,* IX, 211.)

concerning smiths' forges, showing at large the trouble the
country was in upon that account, and the uncertainty of the
law in it, which was severally construed in several counties
and by several judges.

The House ordered a bill to be brought in to remedy the
abuses of the collectors of hearth money.

Then we read over the bill for the excise upon foreign
commodities, and ordered to debate it tomorrow morning.

Then we went up to a conference with the Lords about our
differing with them in their proviso; the conference managed
by Sir Heneage Finch, Sir Thomas Meres, and Mr. Coleman.

Friday [March] 3[5]

THE Lords sent down word that they did agree with us in
leaving out their proviso concerning their houses of peers not
to be broken up but in the presence of one of the commissioners.

Then the Lords sent word they desired a conference about
the address concerning popery, which conference was agreed
to. At the conference they seemed to agree to the thing as
reasonable and fit, and only desired to see the proof of the
matter of fact alleged by the House of Commons.

The Commons ordered the reasons given by Mr. Attorney
General and the rest that managed that conference to be in-
serted in their journal.[6]

Saturday [March] 4[7]

THE House turned into a grand committee to proceed upon
the bill of excise upon foreign commodities, having first resolved to alter the method of collecting the duty from the
first buyer as now it stands, and make it payable by the merchant importer, which will save all the charge of collecting

5. Omitted in Grey.   6. *C.J.*, IX, 212.
7. Omitted in Grey, but see above, p. 85, n. 1.

it, for it will thus be done at the custom house and by the same officers, and will save also half the bill, in length, at least, which consists in a clause adapted to the collection of it from the first buyer, and for preventing frauds of that nature.

Memo: All the merchants of the House seemed to be well content to have it payable by themselves, which may seem a paradox at first, since now they must lay down a great deal more money than otherwise they needed to have done, and that even before they sell their commodity. To which I think the true answer is this, that the merchants of the House are all rich men and of great stock, and will not suffer by laying out a little more money upon their first return, for they will find their advantage in it:

1. Because they shall have ten per cent discounted for what part of the duty they shall pay down in ready money before the time the duty is payable, which will be 9 months.

2. Because this will beat out all the young traders of small stock, who will not be able to advance money as the others can do, and so in a great measure keep the trade in the hands of those men who now have it.

Monday [March] 6[8]

THE Lords sent down the bill for ale and beer with an amendment leaving out the clause for repealing the penalties and prices of former laws.

This the House did disagree with their Lordships, though for my part I thought it very just and necessary that some certain price should be set, and which they should not exceed, and not leave ale to the discretion of alehouse-keepers and victuallers. I spoke at large to it, and much of the sense of the House went that way, but it was carried against it:

1. Because agreeing with the House which was the proper question, would not do it, because that had established the

8. Omitted in Grey.

former prices of 1*d*. per quart strong beer, and a half-penny small, which all confessed to be too low, by reason of the excise.

2. Because the Lords' amendment* being wholly to leave out a clause in our bill, we could not agree to their amendment with an addition, as we could have done if they sent us down any new clause.

The Lords sent us down also a proviso at the end for the importing [of] beer from the Isle of Man without paying custom, which we did not agree to.

Then we desired a conference with the Lords upon the bill, which was granted presently, and our reasons sent up by our members why we did disagree; viz.:

1. That the prices set by the former statutes were unreasonable and unpracticable even before the excise imposed, and therefore much more now.

2. That the price of barley being uncertain, we could set no certain price on beer.

3. That restraining the prices of beer would lower the price of corn.

It were very easy to answer all these arguments, but the Lords sent us down presently word that they did agree with us, and indeed there was a better reason for agreeing than any of the former, which was that the King was in person in the Lords' House ready to pass several bills, and expected to have this finished that it might be passed at this time.

The Lords agreed also to leaving out their proviso for the Isle of Man.

Whereupon all things being agreed, the Black Rod came down and told us the King commanded our attendance in the Lords' House, whither we presently went; and the King being there before us, in his robes and his crown upon his head, the royal assent was given to 8 public bills [and] 16 private bills. And the King thanking us for our good affections shown to him in these two bills desired us to hasten the dis-

* *Lords' amendment . . . any new clause* underscored in MS.

patch of what other public bills were before us that there might be a recess towards the end of the month.

The House had this day a long debate concerning the defaulters, of whom about 18 were ordered to be sent for in custody and to be heard at the Bar of the House before they took their places, and this was effectually done by Mr. Thomas before he was admitted. It was moved in behalf of Colonel Norton that he might not come to the Bar, but to his place and there make his excuse, upon which the House divided and it was carried he should be heard in his place and not at the Bar, and no other reason given for this partiality but that we are masters of our own orders.

To which it was well said by SIR CHARLES HARBORD that we are masters of our orders indeed, but we are servants of our honor, and obliged to preserve that which we should not do if we made such solemn orders one day and revoked them another, especially after we had put them in execution against some persons and then lay them aside as unreasonable against others in the very same case.

But this being passed, the House then revoked the order against all other defaulters, so they are now every one to take his place, and speak for himself if he be called to do so (which it is likely he will not be), and we are bound to believe whatsoever a member shall affirm of his own knowledge, though in his own case, so that there is an absolute end of all punishment of defaulters.

SIR JONATHAN TRELAWNY tendered a bill after one of the clock for removing the assizes of Cornwall from Launceston to Bodmin; and the question being put whether the bill should be now read, it was carried in the negative.

Then SIR THOMAS MERES and SIR CHARLES HARBORD, both very knowing in the order of the House, pretended this bill could be offered no more this session, and that "now" related to this session, not to the time of day, the debate having gone upon the unreasonableness of bringing in new bills now the session was near an end. But the House did not take it so, but restrained "now" as we usually understand it to this day, so that the bill may be tendered again if they please.

Then the House resolved that after Wednesday this week we will sit forenoon and afternoon to dispatch the business before us, that we may rise by the time his Majesty has intimated to us; that is, towards the end of this month.

Memo: This day[9] a great question was agitated in the House whether we ought to receive any petition from without doors relating to anything [which] is done or doing within, and very many spoke against it, and of the inconvenience that may arise of it.

As many spoke of the reasonableness of doing it, the convenience of having information from those that are concerned; the unreasonableness of having that information and those petitions after the things are passed the House, and so out of our power to remedy; and above all the constant practice of the House to receive them, there being, as I think, no assembly in the world which does represent the people which do not also receive petitions from them. And this very parliament has made a law to regulate the manner of presenting petitions, which does admit the rights of the thing. And the inconvenience is not so great as is imagined, for if the petition be unfit for the matter totally, or scandalous in the expressions of it, it is at the peril of the discretion of the member who presents it.

At last the petition was received, being a petition from the refiners of sugar in London, and concerning the rates now to be imposed upon sugar imported.

Tuesday [March] 7[10]

SHROVE TUESDAY. The House did sit though many voted against sitting this day.

We entered upon the bill for foreign excise, and Mr. Sey-

9. This debate actually occurred on Saturday, March 4.
10. Omitted in Grey.

mour being in the chair of the committee, the first particular we entered upon (having postponed the preamble and the next clause which had a blank for the time from which the bill should begin, and when it should end) was Spanish tobacco which stood in the bill six pence per pound new duty, which the committee reduced to four pence. Then of Virginia and other tobacco of the English plantations, which stood at 3*d.* per pound, and the debate ran altogether whether we should reduce it to two pence or to a penny, and the major part of the House seemed to be for a penny, but Mr. Treasurer standing up and pressing for 2*d.,* and Sir George Downing for a penny, when the question was going to be put, Colonel Birch moved for 3 half pence, which being seconded by Sir Thomas Meres, two pence no longer insisted upon, and the question for 3 half pence was put and carried.

Memo: A question being asked whether we could hear the Virginia merchants then at the door against this imposition, it was agreed by all that we being now* in a grand committee of the House could not call any persons in, nor receive any petitions or papers, but such as had been ordered by the House to be received.

Then Sir William Thompson stood up and declared there was an order of the House to hear the Virginia merchants and made upon his motion. So we searched the books and could find no such order. Then he averred he had read it in the minutes, and it was the clerk's fault he had left it out in the order. Then a dispute arose concerning the authority of the minutes, and some said what was there was an order, and Sir Job Charleton and others denied those notes to have the force of orders. However, to satisfy ourselves, and in respect to the member affirming it, we did search the minutes, and there no such thing did appear as he affirmed, only some general words at the end of the order, which we did all take to concern only the planters of sugar, not those of tobacco.

* *Now in a . . . to be received* underscored in MS.

So that to end the matter, we desired the Speaker to take the chair, and that Mr. Seymour should desire* the House to give the grand committee leave to hear the merchants concerned in the Virginia trade; which being asked by Mr. Seymour in the name of the committee, and granted, the Speaker immediately left the chair and Mr. Seymour took it, and the merchants were called in and heard.

Memo: They were heard by Mr. Offley and another which they had retained as their counsel, which seemed extraordinary, and is new to hear counsel only of one side, no party concerned to oppose or answer them, and no point of law at all in the case. And indeed they said nothing which every member of the House did not know before, and which had been said over and over in the House.

Memo: It was said by Mr. Jones that if a pair of shoes of 2s. or half a crown be carried out of England into Virginia the return for that into England is thirty pound of tobacco, which pays already 5s. to the King by the duty of 2d. per pound already imposed, which shows the vast advantage we have by that trade, the customs of this only commodity bringing to the King yearly above 80,000l.

[Wednesday March] 8

Being Ash Wednesday the House did not sit.

Thursday [March] 9[11]

The House sat in the forenoon and afternoon, and soon after their sitting turned into a grand committee to proceed upon the bill of foreign commodities, and voted many of them, the chief debate was upon sugar, which is settled at a farthing per pound on brown sugar of our own plantations, and a penny upon white, both our own and Portugal's.

* *Desire the House . . . the Virginia trade* underscored in MS.
11. Omitted in Grey.

Friday [March] 10[12]

WE proceeded in the same method; the most material thing was salt which was brought in at *2d.* per gallon the foreign salt, (except Scotch salt) which the committee reduced to one penny.

Memo: Yesterday being the 9th, the House of Commons sent up to the House of Lords to desire a conference, and before the return of our messengers we adjourned the House, which was certainly an oversight, for if the House of Lords had agreed to a present conference, we had been gone and could not have met, which they would have complained on and had reason, there having been never any such example; and I spoke afterwards to several ancient parliament men who confessed it slipped by them; but as it happened all was well, for the Lords, engaged in a long debate, did not appoint the conference till next morning.

Saturday [March] 11[13]

WE proceeded in the forenoon upon the bill against popery, and whereas it was first directed that all officers should take the oaths of allegiance and supremacy, it was now added they should take a third oath; viz., that against taking up arms against the king or those commissioned by him.

A proviso was tendered by MR. MILWARD that nothing in this new act should extend to such papists whose lands had been sold by the late usurped power.

But it was rejected because this bill does not much concern the papists by any new penalties, but the forfeiture of two thirds of their estate, which is that the proviso would prevent it by former acts. And the bill, being engrossed, was put to the question and passed.

In the afternoon we sat upon the bill for foreign commodities, and made some progress in it.

12. Omitted in Grey.   13. Omitted in Grey.

Monday [March] 13[14]

In the morning both Houses attended his Majesty in the Banqueting House in Whitehall with our address against popery to which the Lords had agreed. The King said he would take care in it and send out his proclamation to that purpose.

Then we spent the rest of the forenoon upon the bill of indigent officers, and sent up to the Lords to demand two conferences, but by several messengers, one by Sir Thomas Meres and the other by Sir John Talbot. The Lords agreed to both presently, the one to begin as soon as the other was over in the Painted Chamber.

In the afternoon we proceeded upon the bill for foreign commodities, and went through it; and then went through the corn clause brought in by Colonel Birch; and then we entered upon the clause for taking off the imposition of 8s. per caldron upon Newcastle coal and other coal, and the question was whether we should raise it to this bill or leave it to a bill by itself, and the committee dividing upon it, it was carried to add it to this bill.

Tuesday [March] 14[15]

We proceeded again upon the coal clause, and voted that 1s. per ton should be paid for all coal exported in English shipping, and 8s. per ton for what is exported in foreign shipping.

It was much argued that we should put but a very small duty more upon foreigners than upon our own exporters, because that would manifestly increase the export of coal, but it was answered the intent of this clause was not so much to export coal and so to benefit these few persons who have the coal mines, but to breed up a nursery of seamen, which is more done by the coal trade than any other whatsoever, for the merchant ships trading to foreign parts seldom or never

14. Omitted in Grey.   15. Omitted in Grey.

take in any boys to breed them up to be seamen, which the colliers constantly do.

[Wednesday March] 15[16]

[Thursday March] 16[17]

WE proceeded upon the same bill, and went through it, or very near; there remaining nothing but that of brandy, which we could not well tell what to do in. We had already left it out of the ale and beer bill because we knew we could meet with it in this bill; and* in this bill we had been upon it several times, and could come to no resolution, though everybody thought it absolutely necessary to do something in it, either to prohibit or else to lay so great an imposition upon it as may encourage our own making it in England of our own corn.

The difficulty we lay under was how a bill for the prohibiting of brandy which lay before the Lords, sent up to them by the Commons April last, which being this sessions, we could not properly entertain any bill of the same nature while that is depending there; nor could we desire a conference with the Lords upon it, because a conference is always desired by the House where the bill remains, not by them who sent up the bill; nor could we take notice of the aversion of the Lords from passing the bill or any arguments used by their Lordships against it, for that were a breach of privilege; and to send messages from us to put them in mind of that bill lying before them was proper enough, but it was very useless; we had done so often, but they would never send us any answer;

* In the MS. a line is drawn down the margin from *and in this bill* to the end of the entry for the day.

16. In the MS. the dates 15 and 16 are written side by side in the margin, but it is probable that the debates reported under those two dates occurred on the 16th. Grey omits the 15th.

17. Grey reports the petition of the governors of the corporation of the poor.

and to put a high imposition upon brandy in this bill, when we had a bill depending before the Lords of our own sending up for a total prohibition of it, seemed of all other things the most irregular and unprecedented; and thus it stood with us a long time. But at last, there being an absolute necessity to do something in it, we consented, as I may call it, to forget the bill we had in the Lords' House (of which we found we could have no finish), and to put it in this bill as a prohibited commodity, and with an additional penalty of 30 per cent *ad valorem* upon any man that should bring it in besides the forfeiture of the goods.

Friday [March] 17[18]

WE entered upon the report of the bill of foreign commodities to the House, and agreed with the committee in most things. But as we were going on, the Lords sent down the long expected bill of brandy, but with so many amendments that we were forced to put off consideration of them till the next day.

The bill for foreign commodities being upon division of the House carried to continue for nine years, my LORD RICHARDSON moved this day to add a tenth year for the payment of the many debts contracted between February 1660 and the end of May 1660, and was seconded by COLONEL BIRCH and SIR THOMAS LITTLETON.

But this was not at all liked by the House, for the nine years was carried by a question, and contrary to the expectation and desires of many who thought six years had been enough for this as well as for the excise of ale and beer.

Then it was urged by SIR THOMAS MERES that we had no other debt before us but the 1,300,000, of which this was no part, and so could not properly be now taken into our consideration.

SIR THOMAS CLERGES desired we would also pay the 3

18. Omitted in Grey.

regiments of horse disbanded in Scotland upon the King's coming in, and upon assurance of being paid all their arrears.

Sir William Lowther desired that all the gentlemen who had lent any money to the King in the late wars might be satisfied.

Sir Thomas Holt that all those who would not abjure the covenant might be taxed towards the satisfaction of those who had suffered for his Majesty.

But all those motions were made by these gentlemen not in earnest, but to show the unreasonableness of the former motion; and, as I easily foresaw, it came to nothing, for the question being put, as of necessity that must be the first question, whether we did agree with the committee, all these who had formerly voted for 9 years would now be sure to vote to agree, for if we should disagree with the committee, then it would be as proper every wit to move to have the time but 6 years as ten.

This day,* it being insisted upon whether the House should sit in the afternoon, and the affirmative and negative put, the question was who should go forth, and it was said the noes must because it was a regular thing for the House to sit.

It was answered to sit in the affirmative was not the course of the House, and therefore the yeas must go forth.

The reason was allowed, but it was answered again that the House had made an order to sit forenoon and afternoon,[19] and therefore now the noes were to go forth, for they were against the order.

It was replied that order was made ten days since and was intended to continue but four days. It was answered no such thing appeared in the order and therefore it did stand till resolved by a new order. It was replied the House sat yesterday in the afternoon by a particular order, which was an intimation that the general order was expired.[20] It was answered

* In the MS. a line is drawn down the margin from *This day* to the end of the entry for the day.

19. *C.J.*, IX, 216.   20. No such order appears in the *Journal*.

that particular order was not for sitting in the afternoon, but for restraining the business of that sitting to a particular debate. It was answered by Sir Richard Temple that the House had avoided their order for sitting in the afternoons because they had adjourned one day since that; viz., on Tuesday last, with noon to next morning being the usual time of sitting, and this being done by the House without question, it was an avoiding and tacit superseding of the former order.

And this seemed to be allowed by the House, but the matter came not to be determined, Sir Thomas Clifford yielding to forbear sitting this afternoon, upon an order that we should go on tomorrow morning the first business with this bill of supply.

Memo: It was said by Sir Thomas Lee, speaking against sitting in the afternoon, that it was unreasonable to sit so, for gentlemen could not attend the House all day long, and we had experience of it by our sitting Wednesday before in the afternoon, when, as he heard, we were but 38 members in all at the adjourning.

The Speaker said it was a great mistake, for he did assure us upon his own knowledge there were about 50 present.

Sir Thomas Lee appealing to some members that were present, Mr. Sacheverell stood up, and said that he and another member did reckon them, and they were but 35.

The Speaker seemed very angry, and said and was seconded by other members that it was very unfit for any member to speak that a day or two after when it was not possible for anybody to contradict them; and if they had observed any such thing they should have mentioned it at the time, that the Speaker might have taken notice of it; and Sir Robert Carr and Mr. Spry said they had reckoned at the same time, and the number present was 48.

However, The Speaker did declare to us that as to the continuance of the parliament it was all one, what number we were, for we could no more dissolve ourselves than we could call ourselves together; and that the consequence is no

more, but that when there are not 40 present, we must stay
till there are, and ought to do nothing with a less number
than 40; but if there were no adjournment, and the Speaker
should leave the chair without saying they adjourned or that
there should not be 40 when the time of meeting does come,
yet the House does continue in being, for we are not a court
of record which is continued by adjournment; and the ab-
surdities would be too great if it were in our power to dissolve ourselves if we did intend to do so, and much more if
we should be dissolved by chance when neither his Majesty
commanded nor we ourselves designed it.

And I am of this opinion, and so, as I think, were the
whole House, and SIR THOMAS LEE answered that he did not
object it to any such purpose as to show the House was dissolved, but only as an argument against sitting in the afternoon when the House was likely to be so ill attended.

Saturday [March] 18[21]

WE sat forenoon and afternoon and went through the bill of
foreign commodities. Safflower we excused from the payments
of any new duty because it was very necessary for dyeing,
and so, consequently, for our clothing trade. And then we
had a third dispute upon iron wire, but at last again excluded
iron wire and brass wire from any new duty. Then we had a
long debate upon the corn clause; whether the allowance to be
given to the King should be to all corn exported or only to
corn exported in English bottoms; and it was by vote restrained to English bottoms, in favor to our navigation.

I did agree with the votes for wire and safflower, but I dif-
fered in this because this was not intended for navigation
properly, but for encouragement of tillage, and benefit of the
much decayed farmers, and no doubt but this will hinder one
half, at least, of the benefit of this clause, for the east country ships which bring timber hither, and are ships made fit

21. Omitted in Grey.

for carrying bulky commodities, and now return home empty, would doubtless have carried away much corn if they had had the encouragement of this act.

In the morning we had a long dispute upon a private bill for a provision for a posthumous son of Sir Henry Yelverton. MR. HAMDEN, SERJ. MAYNARD, SIR JOB CHARLETON, MR. SEYMOUR, SIR JOHN DUNCOMBE, all spoke for the casting it out.

SIR JOHN TALBOT, SIR JOHN ERNLE, SIR JOHN BIRKEN-HEAD, SIR ROBERT STEWARD, SIR CHARLES HARBORD, and MYSELF spoke for the retaining it, and giving it a second reading.

After a long debate the House divided and it was carried for a second reading.

Monday [March] 20²²

WE proceeded upon a bill for the due estreating of recognizances, and to prevent the compounding for them, and upon debate it was committed.

Then we went upon the bill of foreign commodities. The dispute of coal was revived again, and held us very long, and the House divided upon it, and 63 were for not agreeing with the committee, and 82 were for agreeing.

I were one that did agree because, it having been one prevailing argument used to the House to enlarge the time to nine years because we did lower the customs of coal and put the King to some charge upon the exportation of corn, it was not now fair since we had got the 9 years to cast out those clauses.

The next dispute was about brandy, and there we met with divers difficulties which are mentioned here before, and the bill* for brandy being now come down from the Lords though

---

* In the MS. a line is drawn down the margin from *bill for brandy* to *readiest and easiest*, in the next to the last paragraph in this day's entry.
22. Omitted in Grey.

with great amendments and alterations, we had taken obligation now to take notice of it, it being in our House, and upon our table than [*sic*] we had before; yet the amendments the Lords made therein were such as we could by no means assent unto, and yet to declare that before we had read the amendments was most improper, and to delay this new bill of excise till we had read and refused these amendments, and demanded a conference with the Lords upon it, and it was likely a free conference, was at this time very inconvenient, so that every man almost that pretended to know anything of the order of the House moved a several thing.

Among others I moved that we might in the first place insert the clause for brandy in this new bill, which we might regularly do, for it was but disagreeing with the committee who brought in that clause, and then we had one great end which was the hastening of this bill, which might then be immediately ordered to be engrossed. Then we might take up the Lords' amendments, and disagreeing to them as certainly we should do, we should have so much reason on our side, as we need not doubt the Lords would recede from their own amendments, and then we had our end and did certainly secure our orders. Whereas otherwise we must:

1. Reject the Lords' amendments without reading them.

2. Run the hazard of having two bills in the same session, and passed the same day, in law and in fact, for prohibiting the same commodity.

3. Or we must have one bill for prohibiting it, and another for laying an imposition upon it.

4. And must send up the same clause to the Lords in a new bill which they had depending before them in a particular bill, which is altogether unparliamentary.

5. Or we must let the bill, now come down amended from the Lords, be unregarded upon the table, and so fall, which is no ways advisable because the Lords have in their amendments laid an imposition upon the Commons which ought not to pass *sub silentium*.

6. Or we must directly cast out the bill which is now come from the Lords, which, if it were an original bill come down from the Lords, we might do, and questionless were the readiest and easiest way, but being a bill sent up by us, and returned back with amendments, we cannot cast it out now by vote, but the question must be to agree or disagree with the Lords, and upon disagreement to desire a conference.

These difficulties seemed to me very considerable, and to many others, but the desire of doing something in it, and the assurance this bill would pass, which perhaps the brandy bill alone would never do, the Lords having kept it by them ever since April last, made us (I think) pass by all forms, and so vote to agree with our committee, and have a prohibiting clause in this bill; and then ordered to proceed upon the Lords amendments to our former bill tomorrow morning.[23]

Tuesday February 4, 1672[–3][1]

MEMO: This day after several prorogations made; viz., from the 22nd April 1671 to the 16th of April 1672; from thence to the 30th of October 1672; and then again to this present 4th of February 1672, the parliament did meet, and being sent for up to attend the King in the Lords' House, my Lord Chancellor by a great speech bid us go down and choose our Speaker, and present him to the King the next day in the afternoon.

Being come again into the House, MR. SECRETARY COVENTRY moved us to proceed to the choosing of our Speaker, and proposed Sir Job Charleton as a very fitting person in respect of his experience in the order of the House, and long service

23. Dering does not report any of the debates in the House from this date until the prorogation on April 22, 1671. It is probable that he was present at least some of the time, for he was named for committees on March 22, 23, 31, and April 3, 5, 10, 11, 13, and 14. (C.J. IX, 222, 223, 228, 229, 230, 232, 233, 235.)

1. Omitted in Grey.

to his Majesty; which choice was immediately assented to, without any contradiction or dispute; and he having made excuses to the House for his infirmities and insufficiencies for so great a trust, they being not admitted by the House, he was led up to the chair by Sir John Duncombe and Secretary Coventry.

As* soon as ever he was placed in the chair COLONEL STRANGWAYS moved that we would, before all other things, consider the dignity and orders of the House which were much violated by sending out writs in the time of prorogation for election of new members, which were thereupon returned, and did now sit in the House; whereas the custom of the House was that no writs for election should go out in the place of members dead or removed, but by certificate from the Speaker of the House of Commons; and this he desired we might fall presently upon; and this was seconded by SIR THOMAS LEE and MR. HAMDEN and others.

It was said on the other side by MR. SECRETARY COVENTRY, MR. ATTORNEY, SIR JOHN BIRKENHEAD, etc. that we could not possibly entertain any motion at all till we had a Speaker, nor put any question; that we had no Speaker till the King had approved him, which he might either do, or reject him as he pleased; that he was so far from being a Speaker till then, that he ought not to have the mace carried before him, nor so much as to lie before him on the table till that was done, a sure sign that we are not a House.

This was not much contradicted, but SIR THOMAS MERES, and MR. POWLE instanced in the example of 23 Elizabeth, when many members being returned upon writs issued in the prorogation, they were not indeed by order of the Speaker of the House, but by desire of Mr. Treasurer, then, it seems, a principal member of the House, desired to withdraw, and forbear sitting till the case was examined and determined

---

* In the MS. a line is drawn down the margin from *As soon as ever* to the end of the entry for the day.

by the House, and did so,[2] and therefore it was reasonable they should do so now.

It was answered that it is very likely their own modesty would advise them to it, and if they did not, it would be in the power of the House when the Speaker was settled to command them to it; but for the present THE SPEAKER declared he could put no question at all; and after some disputes of this nature came out of the chair without a question.

Some were of the opinion that he could not so much as adjourn the House to meet again tomorrow because that was still a question, and if it were opposed must be determined by division. But it is very incongruous that we should not have power to adjourn from day to day, and the precedents are otherwise as to adjournment.

And MR. HAMDEN said the House had sometime read a bill before the Speaker was allowed by the King, but that was not admitted true; and the books were not looked into to make it out.

Wednesday [February] 5[3]

THIS day in the afternoon the House met again, and about 4 of the clock were called to attend the King in the Lords' House where his Majesty made a speech to us concerning the occasions of calling us together, and my Lord Chancellor enlarged upon it after.

And the Speaker, being approved by his Majesty, returned about 5 into the House, bringing with him the King's speech and my Lord Chancellor's in writing, both which were read in the House; the King's by THE SPEAKER himself, the House sitting bare, the other by the clerk.

Then SIR THOMAS MERES moved to resume the debate of the new elections, but because it was then late, that we should

2. *C.J.*, I, 117. Lord Burghley was treasurer.
3. Omitted in Grey.

not enter into the merits of it, only ordered the gentlemen returned by these writs to be suspended sitting till the matter determined.

Much was said to avoid this vote by THE ATTORNEY, SECRETARY COVENTRY, and SIR JOHN DUNCOMBE; as that suspension of the House was in itself a judgment; that it ought not to be pronounced *partibus manditis;* that it was not necessary at all since we resolved to proceed upon the merits of the case tomorrow morning so that it was impossible they should sit; that their modesty upon yesterday's debate had advised them to withdraw and no need at all of further order; and in truth, I think there was not one of them this day in the House.

But COLONEL STRANGWAYS, SIR THOMAS LEE, BIRCH, SIR ROBERT HOWARD, and MR. SEYMOUR being all for making some vote in it, it was carried, only changing the word "suspension" into "forbearing to sit till the matter [was] determined by the House," and that the House would go upon this question tomorrow morning the first business, and nothing to intervene.

This* being over, SIR PHILLIP MUSGRAVE moved that thanks might be given to his Majesty for his gracious expressions in his speech, which being agreed, and the clerks being not ready at wording it, SIR JOHN BRAMSTON moved that these words might be added to the question "and that we would assist him against his enemies."

This some opposed, because it was a matter of great consequence, and deserved to be well weighed. Others put us in mind of the inconvenience we had formerly run into by our previous votes of standing by the King with our lives and fortunes.

But SIR THOMAS LEE said that it being a matter of weight, and which many would speak to, it being now darkish if we would proceed in it, we must first put the question for can-

---

* In the MS. a line is drawn down the margin from *This being over* to the end of the entry for the day.

dles; which was accordingly done, and carried full in the negative.

Then one candle was brought in for the clerk to write the question by, but after this SIR THOMAS MERES, SIR THOMAS LEE, MR. SWINFIN, COLONEL BIRCH, and many others insisted positively that no question at all could be put, nor ever was put after candles refused, but the question of adjournment; and we must have that or none.

MR. SECRETARY, SIR JOHN DUNCOMBE, SIR RICHARD TEMPLE, and MR. MILWARD insisted upon the convenience of having these words added; the reputation it would give the King abroad; the discourse it would make if now it had been tendered, and desired it should be refused; the right that there was of having a question which had been firsted and seconded, put to the question.

But they all insisting upon the contrary we sat full four hours by one candle till there was not one inch of it left, and could not then come to a question but ended in a motion, made by SIR THOMAS OSBORNE, that we should give the King thanks for his gracious speech, and let him know that we would take the matter thereof into further consideration on Friday morning.

As to my own opinion, I think that after candles denied, no new business can be moved; but if that they are upon be easy and admit of no debate, or be ripened by debate fit for the question, it may be propounded; for why else do they bring in one candle, but to write the question; and till that is agreed, any member may speak to the wording of it as he sees cause. And this debate arising about some addition to the question, that was the proper question which ought to have been put, or at least if it had been refused then, to put the previous question; viz. whether that question should be put or not. But this could not be now obtained, and so we rose after having debated four hours at least by one candle, which I believe was never known before. And even they who opposed all questions but that of adjournment as irregular yet when they had a question to their mind, and without the words so much contended for, did allow a question, and passed it accordingly.

Thursday [February] 6[4]

THIS day we proceeded according to our former order upon the validity of the new elections made upon writs issued out by the lord chancellor during the prorogation, and so without any notice given by the Speaker of a vacancy in the House.

It is urged by SIR THOMAS MERES, by MR. POWLE, and by MR. SWINFIN, and MR. GARRAWAY that these elections were illegal and void, but they showed no precedents at all to that purpose, more than that the late practice of the House was that the Speaker should send notice to the lord chancellor of any vacancy; only one precedent in 4th *Caroli* I in case of Hertford was produced where the writ for a new election being granted by the lord chancellor and delivered to Sir Richard Wynn, he kept it two months in his pocket and never executed it. This being complained of to the parliament when they met, they called for the writ in and granted out a new one; and upon this, it being desired that those writs which were yet unexecuted might be avoided, it was yielded to, and the question put, and ordered accordingly.[5]

Then the dispute arose again as warm as before about the writs which were executed, and that being pressed to be avoided also, SIR ANTHONY IRBY first moved that it might be referred to a committee to examine and report the precedents in the case, which was certainly regular and parliamentary.

This was seconded by THE SECRETARY, SIR THOMAS LITTLETON, SIR JOHN DUNCOMBE, THE ATTORNEY GENERAL, SIR

4. Grey's report of this day is similar to Dering's.
5. *C.J.*, I, 921.

RICHARD TEMPLE, SIR THOMAS OSBORNE, and MYSELF, but all in vain.

It was put to the question and the affirmatives for referring were 103, and the negatives were 169.

And after this the main question was put and carried that these elections were void, and that the Speaker should issue his warrants to the clerk of the crown for new elections to be made.

Memo:*

1. That it is certain, regular, and parliamentary to refer such things as concerned the practice of the House, and in which the practice is doubtful and controversial to a committee to inspect precedents and report.

2. That the precedents then mentioned in the House are obscure, but much more tending to justify the power of the chancellor of sending out writs in prorogations than the contrary.

3. That the ancient practice to the end of Queen Elizabeth's reign was undoubtedly so.

4. That the precedent of 23rd of the Queen so much insisted upon is nothing at all for them; the sending out of the writs in prorogation being not at all questioned, but the sending them out in places of members that were living, and only sick or absent.

5. That the precedent 7th *Jacobi* seems full for it, it having been allowed by the House in the case of 24 members then dead, and only questioned in the case of 4 that were removed.[6]

6. That several instances were produced in the latter end of King James, and 3rd and *quarto Caroli*.[7]

7. That the precedents since 1640 can not weigh much, and it was offered by THE ATTORNEY GENERAL that if they

---

* In the MS. a line is drawn down the margin from *Memo* to the end of the entry for the day.

6. *C.J.*, I, 392.

7. On Jan. 22, 1628–9, the whole question of the power of the lord keeper to issue writs was referred to the committee of privileges, but there is no record of their report in the *Journal* (I, 921).

could produce any one instance before 1640 of an election avoided upon that ground, the cause should be yielded unto them.

8. That all the discourse against this thing went upon the consideration of inconveniences which might arise upon this power in the chancellor, which was no proper argument, this being a question of right and not of convenience, and when the right is stated, if the inconveniences be considerable, we must remove them by a law for the future, for everything was not a privilege which we desired or thought useful; that, at least, this had been a question disputed between the parliament and the chancery this 100 years, and not to be determined by a too hasty vote, since it was plain that not long since the very clerk of the crown had claimed the privilege of sending out writs *ex officio,* even without any order either from the Speaker or from the lord chancellor, and a report did appear of 46 such writs made out by the clerks in Queen Elizabeth's time in time of prorogations, two even in time of adjournment.[8]

Friday [February] 7[9]

THIS day, in the first place, we settled the committees according to custom, and in the first place the committee of elections, which though it be a select committee, yet it was agreed ought to be settled before the grand committees; the reason being, as I take it, because before all things the House ought to be right settled in the number and due election of its members, as the foundation of all other things. The committee for elections could not be revived because it was now a new session, which is in nature of a new parliament, and was therefore named anew; which were about 60 in number, and ordered to sit on Tuesdays, Thursdays, and Saturdays, and

8. See *C.J.,* I, 927.
9. Grey's report of this day is similar to Dering's.

to meet first in the Exchequer Chamber. Then the grand committees were ordered to sit.

After this we went upon the King's speech according to order, and SIR THOMAS DOLEMAN, in a set oration, laid forth the necessity of undertaking this war, and the present management of it, the little expense it had been hitherto, and concluded with a motion for a supply for his Majesty of 70,000 per mensem for 18 months, amounting in all to 1,260,000.

This was well received by the House, but SIR THOMAS MERES stood up and spoke long, glancing at the clause in the declaration by which the King does suspend or abrogates several acts of parliament; and that kings did usually consult with their parliament before they engaged in a war; at least he did expect that some of the privy council would open to us the motives and occasions of this war; and that then he should be willing as any man to supply his Majesty; but he could not but mind them that it was not regular* nor parliamentary to vote any sum of money in the House, but the *quantum* and the *modus* were still first debated in a grand committee where everyone had liberty of speaking often, which was very necessary in such occasions as these; and therefore moved we might go into a grand committee, only first with a previous† vote of the House that we would supply the King suitable to his occasions and the present necessities of the kingdom.

This was seconded by some, and many would have had that the last clause of the previous vote [be] left out.

Then MR. SECRETARY stood up and gave us a very full and well expressed narrative of the grounds of the war; of the insolence, affronts, and injuries of the Dutch at the treaty of Breda and since. Which having pleased the House, it was thought best to go immediately into a grand committee without contending for the previous vote, which was indeed most

* *Regular nor parliamentary . . . a grand committee* underscored in MS.
† *Previous vote . . . of the kingdom* underscored in MS.

regular; and the Speaker leaving the chair, Mr. Seymour took the chair of the committee.

Mr. Garraway presently moved that, to show their loyalty to his Majesty, and their readiness to supply him against his enemies, we might grant him a supply for 18 months according to the proportion of the royal aid, which was something less but very near 70,000 per mensem. Which, being seconded by Mr. Strangways and Sir Thomas Meres, passed immediately, *nemine contradicente,* and so reported back presently from the committee to the House, was by them confirmed and a bill ordered to be brought in on Monday for it.

Sir John Holland offered to their consideration the inequality of the proportions upon the several counties, and instanced particularly in Norfolk, but the House was so zealous that this supply might be speedy and useful to the King that they would give no ear to anything that might obstruct or delay it.

Saturday [February] 8[10]

A bill was tendered for making the stealing of children felony and read the first time.

The House was moved by Mr. Cheyney to order a bill to be brought in for naturalization of Dutch Protestants.

It was moved by Sir George Downing that it should be to all Protestants.

It was moved by Sir Thomas Higgons and Sir Charles Harbord that it might extend to all people, and not to be restrained to Protestants.

But at last it passed that the instructions to the committee should be to bring in a bill for naturalization of all foreign Protestants.

Then was moved by Mr. Garraway that a bill might be brought in for abating of strangers' customs on goods exported from hence; which was ordered to be brought in.

10. Grey reports a short discussion of the Declaration of Indulgence.

Then was moved in behalf of Sir Roger Bradshaw that his servant had been arrested on the 12th of January last, being in time of privilege, and had indeed made his escape, but dare not now follow his occasions for fear of the bailiffs. Some question was moved in this case, whether this was in time of privilege or not, being 22 days before the day of our session, and so depending upon the old debate whether our privilege began 20 or 40 days before the sitting.

The House would not declare themselves in the point, but ordered the man arrested to be set at liberty, if he be in hold, if not, all proceedings against him to cease during our sitting; and the bailiff that arrested him, and the attorney that was employed in it, to be summoned to attend the committee of privileges.[11]

Then a complaint of SIR ROBERT DILLINGTON, that he was served with subpoena in person eight days before the session, and that the person who served it knew him to be a parliament man.

Ordered that he who served the subpoena be sent for in custody, and the matter examined by the committee of privileges, the first sitting.

Then a complaint from SIR CHARLES SEDLEY that himself and his servant were sent to the counter by a constable but three days before the parliament did meet.

Ordered that the constable be sent for in custody, and to answer his contempt at the committee of privileges.

After this MR. CROUCH moved that we would consider the King's speech; that part in particular which concerned his declaration, which was fit to be thought upon; and only lost it in general terms.

Then it was moved by MR. GARRAWAY that we would begin it by reading again the King's speech.

MR. SECRETARY that the time was late in the day; none

11. The duration of privilege was not fixed by statute, but in practice it was forty days. See T. E. May, *A Practical Treatise on the Law, Privileges, Proceedings, and Usages of Parliament*, pp. 117–120.

of the King's counsel-at-law here; that it was fit to have it done deliberately.

SIR JOHN DUNCOMBE and SIR RICHARD TEMPLE [spoke] to the same purpose.

SIR THOMAS CLERGES moved that we might read the King's speech now, and then adjourn the debate till Monday, which SIR THOMAS MERES closing with, it was so ordered, and the King's speech being read, the House presently adjourned till Monday morning.

SIR ROBERT HOWARD moved for a bill for prohibiting the importation of foreign brandy, which was ordered to be brought in accordingly.

Monday [February] 10[12]

THIS day according to order we were to take into consideration the King's declaration concerning tender consciences, and that clause particularly which did declare all the penal laws in matters of religion to be suspended.

THE SPEAKER put them in mind of the debate adjourned to this day, and for long time no man stood up at all to speak.

At last SIR GEORGE REEVES stood up, and said he perceived that those gentlemen that were so warm for this debate on Saturday were now grown cool in it, and therefore desired the House would proceed to something else.

Then SIR THOMAS MERES stood up, and said though they were willing to proceed very calmly in this business yet they should find they were not cool in it, though there be always too many gentlemen in this House that are but luke-warm in matters of religion, or to that effect; words that from another man would not have passed without some exception taken to them.

But he moved nothing at all, and again a long silence was in the House, till at last SIR THOMAS LEE moved for reading the King's declaration, which was to be the subject matter

12. Dering's report of this day's activity is fuller than Grey's.

of the debate; which was done and after that a long and unusual silence in the House a third time, till THE SPEAKER
putting them in mind that time was precious, and it was now
half past eleven, my LORD CAVENDISH then stood up, and
desired that the reasons of the House given to his Majesty
upon the like occasion in March 1662 might be read, which
being seconded by SIR JOHN MOUNSON, was done, and those
reasons read, which were indeed direct to the matter in hand,
and full against all indulgence to dissenters in religion; one
reason among others being that there were laws of uniformity
in force, which could not be dispensed with but by act of parliament, and that his Majesty's declaration from Breda, or
any otherwise, could not bind him against the advice of his
people tendered in parliament, with other things to this purpose.

Then MR. WALLER stood up and made a long premeditated
speech concerning the power of the King in ecclesiastical
matters; the usefulness to the people of his power of dispensing, instanced particularly in the dispensing of keeping of
Lent, which because it pleased us, we did not complain of.

Then MR. POWLE made a long speech to the contrary,
showing that the King could not dispense, much less suspend,
the laws in being.

MR. SEYMOUR, SIR ROBERT HOWARD, and SIR GEORGE
DOWNING spoke for the declaration. COLONEL STRANGWAYS,
SERJEANT SEYS, and MR. WHORWOOD and SIR THOMAS
MERES against it.

MR. ATTORNEY GENERAL opened at large the* King's
power in ecclesiastical matters; that it was the same with what
it was in temporal; that his supremacy as head of the church
was chiefly negative, and exclusive of all others, particularly
of the Pope, and so it was put in the 39 Articles, and so in the
oath of supremacy; that the convocation could make no canons
without the King's consent, and yet even then they did not
bind without authority of parliament; but that in particular

* *The King's power . . . exclusive of all others* underscored in MS.

cases the King might judge of the expediency of many laws, and dispense with them *pro bono publico;* that he might pardon the penalties of any laws after they were broken was known by all; that in many cases he might dispense with the law before it was broken, as in the act of navigation, when we wanted provisions to set out our fleet, and could not have them but in foreign bottoms, he had done, and with very just reason; and in the act for planting hemp and flax he had done in Ireland; and in the case of the act for the breadth of cart wheels, made this very parliament.

But the debate quickly went off from justifying and maintaining the clause to the manner of laying it asleep; the words of the question moved by many being that we should vote it illegal. Others, thinking that too harsh, would have us proceed by petition to the King that he would be pleased to consider the consequences of those words; that they gave us some apprehensions of invalidating our laws without the due proceedings which we conceive ought to be by acts of parliament; and that he would please to declare that the laws in matters of religion and uniformity were still in force, notwithstanding the said declaration; and for the wording of it, it might be done with more respect to his Majesty, and with more full security of what we desired by a petition than it could be done by a vote; and therefore moved that a committee might be appointed to draw up such an address to his Majesty. This was moved by SIR ROBERT CARR, seconded by MR. SECRETARY, MYSELF, MR. ATTORNEY GENERAL, and SIR THOMAS OSBORNE; but opposed by SIR THOMAS MERES, SIR THOMAS LEE, SERJEANT SEYS, and others.

That which I said was to this purpose: that we were told on all sides that this was a very nice question, and so indeed it was; that many a good man there, and desirous to do his duty to his King and his country, might yet be very doubtful what to advise them to; that I was no advocate for that clause in the declaration which was now under debate because that I did not see any material difference between an universal indefinite, unlimited suspension of laws, as this seemed to be by the declaration, and a total repeal and abrogation, which no man had yet affirmed the King had power to do. But yet I did most willingly join with these gentlemen who had made it their desires that it might be suffered at least *decenter cadere;* that there might pass no vote upon this occasion which might so much as in appearance lessen the entire happy harmony that was between the King and this House; that if we did look back what our ancestors had done in this place, it might be some directions to us what to do; that I should not look further back than to 3rd *Caroli,* a parliament that was zealous enough for the liberty of those who sent them thither, and which had been already often cited in the debates of this day. They had then many reasons to complain of the viola- tion of their laws, and in matters of supreme importance; the imprisonment of their persons in the case of Heveningham;[13] the banishment, under pretences of foreign employment, in the case of Heyman and Glanville;[14] commissions of mar- tial law granted, and executed too; and some suffered by them. That yet all this produced but a petition and address commonly known by the name of the Petition of Right; and that secured them. That thanks be to God the case was now very different, no man could yet say that anyone's liberty or property had been invaded in the least, or that suffered to the value of a hair of his head. That what we complained of was rather what we feared than what we felt; that I would not deny but these fears were worthy of our consideration by men in the trust under which we were, but I would not have any jealousy from a doubtful word or unweighed expression put us upon anything that might be inconvenient or so much

13. Sir John Heveningham was one of the defendants in the case of the Five Knights.

14. In 1622 Sir Peter Heyman spoke against the King's demand for a loan. As a punishment he was ordered to attend Lord Chichester, and to make the journey at his own expense. Sir John Glanville, who in 1625 pre- pared a protest against the dissolution of parliament, was sent with the fleet to Cadiz as secretary to the council of war.

as ungrateful to his Majesty. That we all agreed in the end, and I, as much as any man, aimed at the security of our laws, only debated about the means of coming to it. That it was yet but 4 days since Mr. Speaker had, in the name of the House, desired leave of his Majesty to address ourselves to him in all cases of difficulty and importance; that I did not know any case more important likely to happen than this, and therefore thought it proper to make use of that liberty we had asked and his Majesty had granted; that from so gracious a King to so dutiful and loyal a parliament we could no ways doubt of a satisfactory answer; and therefore humbly moved them to name a committee to draw up an address to his Majesty upon the subject matter of this debate.[15]

At last, the question being stated and called for, it was moved that the previous question should be put; viz., whether the question should be put or not. And the House being divided, the yeas that stayed in were 168, the noes that went out were 116.

After this the main question was put in these words, "whether the penal statutes of this kingdom in matters ecclesiastical can be suspended otherwise than by act of parliament," and carried full in the negative without dividing the House. Then they ordered a committee to draw up an address to the King upon this vote and the debate of the House. And Tuesday being Shrove Tuesday and Wednesday Ash Wednesday, the House adjourned to Thursday.

Thursday [February] 13[16]

THE bill for regulating elections of parliament men was read the second time and committed.

A motion made by MR. POWLE in behalf of Mr. Bertie, who complained against the election of Mr. Gwyn, was referred

15. For Grey's report of Dering's speech see *Debates*, II, 24.
16. Omitted in Grey.

to the committee of elections; and they ordered to sit this afternoon, having not yet sat at all.

Then the bill for the 18 months tax was brought up by MR. ATTORNEY GENERAL, but before that was read SIR THOMAS MERES moved the House that the gentlemen commanded to draw up the address to the King by the vote on Monday might withdraw and agree upon it; which we were ordered to do accordingly.

Mr. Powle was put into the chair of the committee where, after 4 hours debate, we agreed the address, and ordered him to report it to the House next day.

Friday [February] 14[17]

THIS day MR. POWLE tendered the address to the House, which was well received and approved, and a vote passed to agree with the committee, which was said to be the regular question.

But then it was moved to add that we would pass a vote that a bill should be brought in for giving ease to dissenters in matters of religion, which they said would very much please his Majesty, to let him see that we did not dislike the matter of his declaration but the manner, and did not doubt the prudence but only the legality of it. This the House seemed inclined to do, but in debate many questions were started; many inclining to have no vote at all but send the address as it is; many would have no vote as to the matter, only a vote that on Monday morning to consider what ease was fit to be given to these dissenters; and of this opinion I was myself, and was seconded in it by SIR ROBERT HOWARD, MR. MILWARD, MR. CHEYNEY, SIR JOHN KNIGHT, and others.

But most were for resolving beforehand and immediately what should be the subject matter of the bill and how far the extent of indulgence should go. And upon that all the debate

17. Grey's report of this day's activity is fuller than Dering's.

was whether the word "Protestant" subjects should be in the question or not, which held very long, and was maintained by MR. GARRAWAY, MR. SWINFIN, COLONEL STRANGWAYS, and SIR WILLIAM COVENTRY, and others. Many others spoke to have it left at large to the committee, and some expressly that papists as well as others should be indulged.

At 2 of the clock the question was put, whether a bill should be brought in for ease to his Majesty's Protestant subjects, dissenting from the Church of England, and passed in the affirmative *nemine contradicente.*

Then it was resolved the House should turn into a committee on Monday morning to consider such a bill.

Then it was moved by SECRETARY COVENTRY to have the concurrence of the House of Lords to this address, which was seconded by SIR CHARLES HARBORD, and SIR THOMAS OSBORNE, and opposed by others. This debate held very long, and at last came to a question upon which the House divided, and 110 for sending to the Lords for their concurrence, and 125 against it.

Memo: I were not in the House at this question.

Memo:* It is usual to desire the concurrence of the Lords in things of this nature; and in the Petition of Right, which much resembles this case, was so. But upon the former declaration in 1662, the Commons went alone; and having now voted this vote concerning a bill for ease of dissenting Protestants to be brought in, and the Speaker to take notice of it to his Majesty, they could not properly join with the Lords; that being not proper for us to communicate to the Lords, nor for the Lords to take notice of to the King.

Saturday [February] 15[18]

THIS day about eleven of the clock Mr. Speaker came to the House sick, having been forced that morning to be let blood;

---

* This whole paragraph underscored in MS.
18. Omitted in Grey.

which being taken notice of, SIR JOHN DUNCOMBE, as soon as he was in the chair, moved him for his own health's sake that he would take a little time of ease, and therefore that he would adjourn till Tuesday; which was done immediately.

Tuesday [February] 18[19]

THIS day, the House being met, and the Speaker continuing sick, MR. SECRETARY COVENTRY moved us to choose a new Speaker,[20] and recommended to us MR. EDWARD SEYMOUR for that purpose, who, being presently agreed upon, took the chair in his sword and belt, a thing hardly ever seen before in that place. Soon after the Black Rod came to command us to wait upon his Majesty in the House of Lords, where Mr. Seymour was approved by his Majesty, and confirmed our Speaker, who then, coming back to us, put on a black velvet gown with gold buttons ready prepared for the occasion.

Then the House gave the bill of subsidy a second reading, and ordered it to be committed. Much debate there was when the committee should sit upon it, MR. SECRETARY COVENTRY proposing Thursday and SIR THOMAS MERES Saturday. At last SIR ROBERT HOWARD proposed Friday, which was agreed to.

Several motions were made for altering the proportions of the taxes, SIR JOHN HOLLAND for Norfolk, SIR JOHN BRAMSTON for Essex, SIR HENRY FELTON for Suffolk, and MR. WESTPHALING for Hereford, but none were assented to, but only London, which was recommended to the committee to consider of by reason of their great suffering of the plague, the fire, and the war.

I said nothing for Kent, not that I were unwilling to speak

19. Omitted in Grey.

20. In March, 1606-7 the Speaker fell ill (the etiology of his illness was partly political), and the Commons were uncertain of their right to elect a new one. The matter was referred to the committee of privileges, but before anything was done in the matter the old Speaker resumed his seat. (D. H. Willson, ed., *The Parliamentary Diary of Robert Bowyer*, pp. 240–242.)

for it, or unsensible of its suffering, but I knew it was very ungrateful to the King to make any alterations in the proportions because of the delay it would infallibly bring to the bill; and indeed the former vote had absolutely precluded all debates of this kind, and settled not the sum only but the proportions also. So I thought not fit to move till some one county had broken the way, and then it would be more regular, and more likely to succeed.

Wednesday [February] 19²¹

THIS day SIR THOMAS MERES moved from the committee of privileges that the persons who had served a subpoena upon Sir Robert Dillington might be pardoned, and the order for taking them into custody by the serjeant be vacated, they having humbly acknowledged their fault, and Sir Robert Dillington being satisfied therewith. But* the House would not forgive them till they did render themselves to the serjeant, though it was confessed they were three in number, very poor men, and likely to be undone by laying in the serjeant's hands at great fees till the committee should hear their business, and then find time to report it to the House, and the House order their discharge.

Then, the Speaker leaving the chair, the House resolved into a grand committee to consider of the materials for the bill for ease of tender consciences, and put Sir Thomas Meres in the chair.

Mr. Hale first moved that since the business was to give ease to the dissenters, it was reasonable first to know what they complained of. This was seconded by Mr. Crouch and Secretary Coventry; and indeed the proper way, but it did not please the House.

Sir John Birkenhead, and Sir Lancelot Lake, and Sir John

---

* *But the House . . . to the serjeant* underscored in MS.
21. Grey's report of this day's debates is similar to Dering's.

Knight spoke, in effect, against any consideration at all of the matter; but the order of the House had before determined that something should be done in it.

At last Sir Thomas Lee proposed that we should begin our debate by consideration of what persons they are that we would give ease unto; that the vote of the House tied us up to Protestants; that among these it was reasonable first to consider those that are nearest our church, for they did most deserve to be eased; and therefore he desired that the persons to be eased might* be such as would subscribe to all the doctrinal articles of the 39, and would take the oath of allegiance and supremacy. This was seconded by Mr. Garraway, Mr. Vaughan, etc.

Much was said against this, as being not proper to the question, which was to ease dissenters, and this [did] not mention any dissenters at all; that in effect, this concerned all people that were Protestants, for this included those who would sign the whole 39 articles, as well as they would sign only 36. If they meant to exclude all those who would not sign the 36 from any ease, then it was much too narrow for the few; if they intended to admit others afterwards, then all the time we should spend upon this question was altogether lost.

However, the words pleased the House, and the question being put whether ease should be given to Protestants that would subscribe the doctrinal articles of our religion and take the oaths of allegiance and supremacy, it passed with very few negatives.

Then fell under consideration what ease should be given them, and it was again asked by some what ease they desired, and whether anybody could undertake to tell us.

Alderman Love stood up and said that he was acquainted with many of them; that he knew they did not desire to be admitted to any offices of honor or profit in the church or kingdom, which was not reasonable to expect without being entirely conformable to the established church; that they did

* *Might be . . . allegiance and supremacy* underscored in MS.

not desire to be exempted from any offices of charge or burden, nor from any taxes or payments to parish duties, nor from tithes, but only from the penalties of the laws made against them; and that they might have leave to worship God in public places to be appointed by the magistrate with the doors open, and, if the House thought fit, in public churches at such times as no other worship or service was there.

This House heard him very well, only this last clause seemed not any ways grateful to them.

At last the question was put only whether such persons subscribing as aforesaid should be eased from any penalties for not going to church, and was carried also in the affirmative.

It was much controverted whether they should have leave to meet for their own worship, whether publicly or privately, but the House could not agree upon it; and it being past one, and the House ordered to meet his Majesty at 3 this day in the Banqueting House, the committee rose.

And the Speaker taking the chair, Sir Thomas Meres reported that the committee had made some progress in the heads of the bill and desired leave to sit again tomorrow.

In the afternoon the House, that is, about 40 members, did meet, and The Speaker, having the address in his hand, asked the House if it were their pleasure he should present it to his Majesty, which he was ordered to do; but first the paper was read. They did not order the Speaker to acquaint his Majesty that we had under consideration a bill for the ease of his Majesty's Protestant subjects dissenting in religion as was their intention when that address was resolved upon.

Then the Speaker went to the Banqueting House where most of the members were gone before, and presented the address to his Majesty, and came back to us in the House, for the House was not adjourned, (and it was said ought not adjourn when they go to the King or to the House of Lords as a House) and reported the King's answer, which was that the business was of importance, and he would consider it.

Thursday [February] 20[22]

THIS day the House proceeded upon their bill for tender consciences in a committee. The debate went not now so much for toleration, as for removing some obstructions which were conceived to lie in the way of many good people who would otherwise come into us; and it was thought fit if we would do no more, we would yet remove the obstructions laid by ourselves this very parliament, and to that end that we would repeal the two clauses in the act for uniformity: one for the assent and consent, the other for abjuring the covenant. It was not thought fit to put them together, but distinctly, and the first was put and immediately carried almost without dispute.

The second part was much controverted, and much said in detestation of the covenant by Secretary Coventry, Colonel Strangways, Sir John Birkenhead, and many others; and indeed the whole House almost showed an aversion to the repealing that clause.

But [it] was moved by Sir Phillip Warwick, and then seconded by Sir William Hickman, Sir John Knight, etc., that we should only repeal that part of this clause which is in these words, "nor upon any other person."[23] It was showed that these were the only words that did give offense; that this form of swearing or declaring was not known in any other oath or asseveration in the world; that it was altogether useless, no man being either bound or loosed by any other man's opinion but his own; that the whole was to expire ten years hence, why not this particular now; that if you would give

22. Grey omits the conclusion of this day's debate.
23. The actual wording is as follows: "And I do declare that I do hold there lies no obligation upon me or any other person from the oath commonly called the Solemn League and Covenant to endeavour any change or alteration of government, either in church or state." (14 Car. II, c. 4.)

anything at all, you could not give less than this, which was of no manner of use or importance to the church to keep in.

This, after a long intermission, was renewed and pressed by Sir William Coventry, Mr. Garraway, and Sir Robert Howard, and thought generally to be the sense of the House, when the question being put, the committee divided upon it, and the affirmatives that these words should be left out were 132, and the negatives 141.

Then Mr. Speaker took the chair again; having given leave to this committee to sit again on Saturday, the House adjourned.

Friday [February] 21[24]

SIR WILLIAM COVENTRY tendered a bill to the House for enabling gentlemen to take apprentices in the trades of cooks, gardeners, and the like, to the age of 24 years, which was read the first time.

MR. POWLE moved the House that a bill might be brought in for preventing of the transportation of wool from England and Ireland, which was ordered to be brought in.

Then SIR JOHN MOUNSON tendered a clause to be added to the bill for the King's supply for allowance to be given by the King for all corn exported into foreign parts, so much per quarter for wheat, rye, barley, and malt. This was not very regular because it was altogether foreign to the bill of supply; and again I had not often observed a clause tendered in the House to a bill after the bill was committed, and before the committee had sat upon the bill, but sometimes at the committee such things had been tendered. THE SPEAKER* took another exception to it, which was that he had not a brief delivered him with it, but that was over-ruled as not

* *The Speaker . . . 3 sheets of paper* underscored in MS.

24. Grey gives only a brief account of the debate on motions to desire an answer from the King to the House's message. This debate actually took place on the following day.

necessary in a clause or proviso, though it be long, as this was, 3 sheets of paper.

After long canvassing of it, it was ordered to be read the second time, and committed with the bill.

Then the Speaker left the chair, and Mr. Attorney took the chair of the committee to proceed upon the bill of supply.

The preamble being postponed as is usual, the first question was upon the first blank, which was the sum to be given to his Majesty, many insisting that it could not be made certain there till the particulars were agreed on in the following proportions of the several counties, and others urging that it was already determined in the House both as to the whole and to the several parts. The only dispute was concerning the proportion of London, which the House had recommended to the consideration of the committee; but since that the lord mayor and aldermen had been with the King, and desired him to consider their necessities and their suffering by the plague, war, and fire, and had received, as it was said, a gracious and satisfactory answer.

Much was said upon this: how unusual it was for any persons to take notice of what was doing in the House before it be done; that they had burgesses here in the House to represent their condition; that it was of ill consequence that any county or city should beg off from the King the proportion taxed upon them by this House; that other counties would follow the example, and had as much reason, so that it must lie at last altogether upon the rest that they had declined the favor intended them by the House, and therefore did not deserve it. But in truth the intention of the House in considering London was not to lessen the King's duty, but to consider what part of the tax of London might be laid upon Westminster and those parts of Middlesex which do lie near to London, and are mightily increased and enriched of late by new buildings, and the trade gone that way since the fire of London.

But this was not insisted upon by the burgesses for London; and the question being put whether London should be eased of part of their proportion, the committee divided, and the yeas were 103, the noes 136.

Then the blank was filled up, and the entire sum agreed, upon which the monthly distributions, and the particular proportions of every county are in effect concluded also; and this was all that was done this day.

Saturday [February] 22²⁵

THIS morning was spent to very little purpose; SIR JOHN HOTHAM moved that this House would desire the members that are of the privy council to move his Majesty to send us an answer to our late address, which was seconded by MR. PALMES, and enforced by SIR THOMAS MERES and MR. VAUGHAN and MR. STRANGWAYS.

It was spoken against by others as not necessary, for the answer would come without it, and as well; that it was not very decent to press the King beyond his convenience; that it was a matter of importance, and it was yet but 2 full days since we delivered it, so that there could be not called any delay as yet in it.

Some heat began to grow in the House by SIR THOMAS MERES saying they were plain country men and could not speak so smoothly as the fine men about the town, but they meant as well to the King as they did; and that he loved to speak plainly, and as they did; and that a gracious answer from the King to this address would very much smooth the passage of the money bill.

This speech was something sharply reflected upon by SECRETARY COVENTRY, as if SIR THOMAS MERES had now and often heretofore labored to make a distinction in the House between the country gentlemen and the courtiers, whereas

25. Grey does not report the meeting of the committee of elections. See above, p. 126, n. 24.

there was none, nor ought to be none; and often used the words "of this side of that House, and that side,"[26] which were not parliamentary, and some things of that nature, but the business was diverted by the House, and so we continued the debate of sending or not sending for an answer.

At last Sir Thomas Lee moved to adjourn this debate till Tuesday morning, which was seconded by Sir Thomas Meres, and others; and so it was ordered without a question; and it being now near one o'clock we thought not fit to go into a grand committee about the bill of religion but adjourned till Monday.

This afternoon I were at the committee of elections. The case was between Mr. Gwyn returned for Chippenham, and sitting thereupon in the House, and Vere Bertie, Esq. who complained of the said election. The matter pretended was corruption; the principal evidence was that Sir Francis Popham, about 40 years since, and Alexander his son gave 12*l.* per annum to be forever distributed among the poor freemen of this town; that is, 40*s.* to six of them yearly; the bailiff and the corporation being always to nominate 12, out of which Sir Francis Popham's heirs were to choose the six who should have this charity. And it was argued, and doubtless true, that some of the electors gave their vote for Mr. Gwyn recommended by the young Sir Francis Popham for their burgess for fear if they should displease Sir Francis Popham they would lose the benefit of this charity. And others, in memory of the kindness this town had received from that family and out of hopes that young Sir Francis would be as kind to the town as his father and grandfather had been, did so also.

But note: here is nothing that does at all reflect upon Mr. Gwyn that he did either give or promise anything, or any man else by his consent, privity, or procurement; which used

26. This is the first evidence which I have seen which shows that members were sitting according to party. But see Trevelyan, *England under the Stuarts*, p. 213.

to be the enquiry in this matter. Here is nothing done or said, given or promised by Sir Francis Popham that is illegal and injurious. The gift of Sir Francis Popham 40 years since can not possibly be so strained, as to be done with design of choosing Mr. Gwyn a member, who was not then born. It is a discouragement upon all people ever to do good to any corporation, since by doing so they exclude themselves and their posterity to the 3rd and 4th generation of being elected by them. And upon the whole it was not possible this corruption could extend to more than six electors, and Mr. Gwyn had a majority of 52, his number being 75, and Mr. Bertie's 23. And if either gratitude for benefits received, or hopes of advantages to come did sway them to give their votes for Mr. Gwyn, it was no more than most men do consider in the persons whom they elect. And at the time of election all things passed very fair and without any exception to any man's vote; only as soon as the election was over Sir Edward Bainton said he believed they should find corruption in it.

Besides* all this, the committee seemed to go beyond their power in hearing any witnesses or words that might reflect on the honor of a sitting member, Sir Francis Popham, he being not mentioned in the petition, nor referred to them by the House. All that was said about Sir Francis Popham's promise to give the town 200 appeared no more than that 4 years since, when the corporation presented a handsome nag to Sir Francis Popham, his father then being there told him, "Frank, this horse will cost you 100*l.* or two, for you must be as kind to this town as I and your grandfather have been," which he said he would be, or to that effect, but had not yet done it, nor since promised it.

But the matter being put to the question it was voted that Mr. Gwyn was not duly elected; the negatives being 76, and the affirmatives 63. Then a second question being put whether Mr. Vere Bertie was duly elected, that was also carried by as many or more votes.

* *Besides all this . . . by the House* underscored in MS.

Something, I confess, might be said as to the former question, though I were in the affirmative, but as to this second vote, I cannot reconcile it by any means to any rules that we have ever owned here, and was totally against it; so at half an hour past ten the committee rose.[27]

Monday [February] 24[28]

THIS day, at the sitting of the House, MR. SECRETARY COVENTRY delivered from his Majesty an answer in writing to our address concerning the suspension of the penal ecclesiastical laws, which being twice read, SIR PHILLIP WARWICK moved we might order thanks to be returned to his Majesty for it, and this was seconded.

But SIR THOMAS LEE standing up said that it was a matter of great consequence; that there were some parts of it which were not very clear, and desired time till tomorrow morning to consider and weigh it; then our thanks would be more considerable when they came from us upon deliberation.

SIR THOMAS MERES spoke to the same purpose; and at last others enlarged further, saying that if we gave thanks for this message we owned every part of it, and yielded up the dispute of the King's power to suspend our ecclesiastical laws, which we had affirmed the King could not do; and the King in his message calls it a power inherent in his crown, and which was never questioned in the time of his progenitors; and the dispute grew still wider.

At last SIR WILLIAM COVENTRY moved that we might give thanks for those expressions of grace and favor which were in it, as certainly there were ·many; and that would not conclude us in these parts we were doubtful of.

This they who were not for giving thanks at all closed

27. The decision of the committee was reversed by the House on March 3, when Gwyn was declared duly elected.
28. Grey gives a full report of the debate on the answer to the King's message but omits any reference to the points of procedure.

with, and now the debate went on this matter, the court side
opposing it, and endeavoring to have indefinite and general
thanks returned. They who would not consent to that would
then have a committee to consider what answer to return to
the King's message, and this was pressed by Mr. Garraway,
Colonel Strangways, Mr. Powle, and Mr. Whorwood,
and others; and this seemed to me much more inconvenient
and dilatory than the other, so at last I ventured to move to
comply with the question as it was stated by Sir Thomas
Meres: that thanks be returned to his Majesty for his gracious assurances and promises in his answer to our address;
and I did truly think that the speed and unanimity of our
thanks [would be] more useful to the King, than the trans-
posing of the words, which was all contended for, and which
we could at best but cover some implied and doubtful sense,
which nobody would think themselves obliged by.

Sir John Duncombe approved that I did, and Sir Phillip
Musgrave seconded it, but that side who had most labored
this, by this time finding their strength, were not now con-
tented with what they had formerly proposed, but were still
urging to have the whole debate committed.

Yet after an hour longer dispute, Sir Thomas Osborne
closing with them upon the words I had consented to before,
it was put to the vote, and carried with very few negatives
that thanks should be returned for his gracious assurances
and promises in his answer, etc. We thought we had now
done, but they would not leave it here but renewed the motion
for a committee to consider further of his Majesty's answer,
which was not very candid, nor indeed regular after one of
the clock, but when that was opposed, they would have the
question for adjourning the debate till Tuesday morning.

This we opposed by reason of its being a motion which
ought not to be entertained at that time of day, and besides,
it was directly against the order of the House which had appointed the money bill for Tuesday morning. And we desired
the question for adjourning the House. This with much ado

was granted us, and though it be a question that seldom miscarries at two of the clock, yet upon the division the yeas for adjourning the House were 123, the noes 142. Then they resumed the debate of the committee to consider the King's answer, but adjourned the debate thereof till tomorrow morning.

Tuesday [February] 25[29]

AT sitting of the House several things concerning privilege and a private bill read for confirming an agreement made by Sir Orlando Bridgman about the estate of Sir Thomas Woolridge.

Then the House proceeded upon consideration of the King's answer to our address, and nominated a committee to draw it up: Mr. Attorney General, Mr. Solicitor General, Sir William Coventry, Sir Thomas Lee, Sir Thomas Meres, Sir Robert Howard, Sir Jonathan Trelawny, Mr. Powle, Sir George Downing, Mr. Secretary Coventry.

Then we went into a committee of the whole House to proceed on the King's supply, and made a good progress in it.

From Wednesday 26 of February to Friday the 7th of March I were absent, being sick.

Friday March 7[1]

THE bill for indulgence to the Protestant dissenters read the second time and committed.

Then a clause was moved to be added to it by way of instruction to the committee; viz., that no dissenters from the established religion should be admitted to sit as members in parliament; and this was pressed by many to be added to this bill. But some saying this was unfit for this bill, others desir-

29. Grey's report of this day's activity is much fuller than Dering's.
1. Grey's account of this day is somewhat different from Dering's.

ing it might be added to the bill against popery, and some
that it should be put in the bill for regulating elections, the
debate was adjourned till Monday morning.

In the afternoon the House waited on the King and presented a petition against the papists.

Saturday [March] 8[2]

WE proceeded in the bill of supply, and went through it, all
but the preamble. But this morning at sitting of the House,
his Majesty sent for the House of Commons up to the House
of Lords, and there in a short but very gracious speech told
them that he did freely and willingly concur to their desire
mentioned in their address the day before presented to him
by both Houses, and that he would suddenly issue forth a
proclamation to that purpose; that he desired they would consider the time of the year, the necessity of setting forth the
fleet very speedily; and that they would proceed with their
bill for supply; that if anything did remain in their minds
concerning his late declaration he did faithfully promise that
what had been lately done should never hereafter be drawn
into consequence or example.

This answer was exceeding pleasing to the House, who
immediately voted thanks to be given his Majesty for his
most gracious, full, and satisfactory answer to their addresses
and petitions given them this day, and desired the Lords to
join with them in it, which they consented to.

MR. SECRETARY COVENTRY then assured them that he had
seen the great seal torn off from the declaration by the King's
command, which the House took great notice of, and expressed themselves well satisfied with.

It was moved by SIR THOMAS MERES, SIR ELIAB HARVEY,
and MR. SACHEVERELL that this information of the secretary
should be entered in the House books, but it was not so ordered; it being said that he did not say this to them as a

2. Grey does not record Coventry's remarks.

message from the King but as a private person only to inform them what he knew.

Monday [March] 10[3]

THIS day we proceeded upon the adjourned debate of the clause for disabling dissenters to be parliament men, and many agreed to have it put into the bill for elections; as MR. GARRAWAY, MR. STRANGWAYS, MR. HALE, MR. MALLET.

Very many would have it [added] to the bill of indulgence; as MR. ATTORNEY GENERAL, MR. SOLICITOR, SIR JOHN BRAMSTON, SIR JOHN BIRKENHEAD, MR. MILWARD, SIR RICHARD TEMPLE, SIR JOHN KNIGHT, etc.

At last I spoke to it; and showing a little the impropriety and inconvenience of putting it to the bill of indulgence, the bill of popery, or the bill of elections, proposed that it might pass in a distinct bill by itself, as the speediest, safest, and most effectual way, and most indifferent of all others when it was neither advantaged nor prejudiced by the contents of any other bill.[4]

This being presently seconded by SIR THOMAS MERES, and soon after by MR. WHORWOOD, and some others, the sense of the House seemed to run that way; and the question being put whether this clause should be an instruction to the committee for the bill of indulgence, the House divided upon it. The affirmatives were 107, the negatives 163.

So this passing in the negative, soon after the motion was renewed by SIR GILBERT GERARD for a bill to be brought in for that purpose, and that was ordered, and SIR THOMAS MERES to bring it in.

Then SIR CHARLES HARBORD made report of some amendments to the bill for preventing the growth of popery, which were read and agreed unto.

Then my LORD CORNBURY tendered a proviso to be added

3. Grey's account is fuller than Dering's.
4. See Grey, *Debates,* II, 96.

to the bill for exempting all the Queen's servants in ordinary, whether natural born subjects of the King or foreigners, from all the penalties and clauses of this bill.

But this the House would not pass, yet in respect did not reject it, but suffered my Lord to withdraw it again, and to amend it, and bring it in again in parliament when the bill is engrossed.

I think all the scruple is upon the words, "his Majesty's natural born subjects," for as to the foreigners, they would not have scruple to allow them.

Then MR. WHORWOOD tendered another proviso to be added, that all people before they had any employment should by an oath abjure the doctrine of Transubstantiation, or praying to the saints, or Virgin Mary, and the infallibility of the Pope, or any council, or any visible church. But much being said against this clause by MR. SECRETARY COVENTRY, SIR THOMAS CLERGES, and others, and all men thinking it too great a matter to resolve so suddenly, they gave Mr. Whorwood leave to withdraw his proviso, and ordered the bill to be engrossed.

Tuesday [March] 11[5]

WE went forward with the bill of supply, and went through it, and ordered it to be reported to the House on Friday.

Wednesday [March] 12[6]

TWO or three private bills read, then the bill against recusants being engrossed, was read the third time. A proviso was offered by MR. WHORWOOD in parchment whereby all persons that were to have any office or employment should abjure the doctrine of Transubstantiation, and swear that in the Sacrament after consecration there remained merely the substances of bread and wine.

5. Omitted in Grey.
6. Grey's account is fuller than Dering's.

This was spoken against by many; SIR JOHN BIRKENHEAD, that no oath was required in Harry VIII or Queen Mary's time, only a confession of their belief; and they were burnt for it, if differing from the then received opinion.

SIR THOMAS CLERGES, that this would give offence to the Lutherans.

SIR CHARLES WHEELER, that the word "merely" was not proper, nor indeed consonant to the expression of the Church of England.

SECRETARY COVENTRY, LORD ANCRAM, SIR ROBERT HOLT, and others [were] against it.

Then SIR THOMAS MERES tendered an amendment to the proviso where instead of "swearing" was put in "should declare and subscribe," and the word "merely" was left out.

This was spoken against as to form, for a proviso tendered in parchment must stand, and just as it is too, and is only capable of some small amendment at the table, but it was ruled here that this proviso as amended by SIR THOMAS MERES should be transcribed anew by the clerk at the table in parchment, and so it was; and then being read it passed, and the bill ordered to be sent up by SIR CHARLES HARBORD to the Lords.

Thursday March 13[7]

THIS day was spent entirely in debating of a proviso tendered by SIR THOMAS MERES to the bill for indulgence. The effect of the proviso was to take away the renunciation of the covenant required by the act of uniformity. He first opening it in general terms, a long debate was upon it, whether it should be read or not, and at last the House divided upon it; 123 were against reading it, and 146 were for reading it.

It being read, it appeared to very many to be too large, and to repeal that renunciation in terms so as to seem to give some

7. Grey's account of this day's debates is fuller than Dering's, but very confused.

countenance to the covenant, which went much against the sense of the House. Yet the question being at last put again, whether it should be read a second time, the noes were 119, and the yeas were 122, so it was read a second time.

For my part, I went out first for it, as believing it grounded upon the debate we had before in the committee, only to avoid the words "or any other person" in the same renunciation, and when I had heard it read, I stayed in against it as thinking it much too large, by repeating that renunciation without any brand of displeasure upon the covenant; and so was the sense of the House.

At last SIR PHILLIP WARWICK offered some other words which agreed well with the sense of the House; but some exception [being] taken to the words of it, the House ordered a committee to draw up a clause to that effect, and then adjourned, having sat till 4 of the clock or very near.

Friday [March] 14[8]

THIS day was spent upon the bill for the King's supply; and going through the amendments, and the commissioners' names took up all the day.

In the afternoon I attended my Lord Berkeley's committee for exchange of the vicarage of Berkeley with the parsonage of Sutton Bonington in Nottinghamshire, which belongs to the dean and chapter of Bristol, being a bill sent from the Lords.

Being at the committee for the highways within parishes of the lines of communication, they put me in the chair.

Saturday [March] 15[9]

THIS day we proceeded upon the few remaining amendments to the bill of supply, which were all agreed; and then the

8. Omitted in Grey.
9. Grey's account is fuller than Dering's.

question for engrossing the bill with the amendments was offered, when MR. HALE of Hertfordshire moved that the bill might lie upon the table till Friday next, which was presently seconded by SIR ELIAB HARVEY, MR. SECRETARY COVENTRY, and SIR JOHN DUNCOMBE; and SIR JOHN KNIGHT moved to them the necessity of a present dispatch, which was opposed by SIR THOMAS MERES, MR. VAUGHAN, and others.

Then MR. WALLER made a long speech to show the necessity which lay upon the King, and that he did not know what consequences might happen from it; that necessity made many things just, which were not so in themselves. MR. SECRETARY COVENTRY spoke to the same purpose and used the phrase of "necessity imposed on the King by this delay."

COLONEL STRANGWAYS and MR. GARRAWAY replied sharply upon this, saying if there were any necessities they were not of our making; that we might have been called together sooner; that if the necessities were such, it was fit to inquire who were the authors of these counsels which had now brought the King to these extremities.

MR. POWLE made a speech showing that we had many grievances to complain of to the King; that our address had comprehended but some few of them; but that it was fit they should be offered to the King before the money bill passed. He instanced in an imposition laid on the subject by order of the council table (I think he meant on coals).

MR. GARRAWAY said there were injunctions lately granted to stop proceedings at law, which were fit to be inquired into, and humbly represented to his Majesty; as also pressing of soldiers.

MR. THOMAS went further, and said it was necessary to remove from the King's presence some dangerous persons about him who were heads of the papist faction; and named the Lord Arundell of Wardour, Colonel Richard Talbot, and Father Patrick; but nobody did second him.

While thus we were running wide from the matter, and into some heat, it was thought best not to reply to any angry words, but to keep as near as we could to the question for engrossing the bill, which was the proper question; and at last this was fixed upon, to move to have the bill engrossed, but that it should be brought in on Friday morning, so that the delay would give them leave certainly to hear from the Lords' House the effect of the bill against popery which we had sent up, and by fixing the third reading of the bill to a certain day there was no room left for surprise, and yet we thought we gained a good point by getting the bill engrossed, and keeping up the reputation in the world that the bill went forward, which would have sunk in the world, if it had been denied to be engrossed.

This was moved by SIR THOMAS STRICKLAND, MYSELF, and seconded by TITUS, SIR ROBERT HOWARD, and after above an hour's debate, at last by SIR THOMAS OSBORNE, and with much ado was consented unto by the other side, with this addition, that it should be brought in on Friday morning engrossed, and not sooner.

SIR THOMAS LITTLETON moved it might be Friday, ten of the clock, and not sooner, which would do the same but sound a little gentler, as seeming to refer to the hour and not to the day; and so it passed.

Monday [March] 17[10]

THIS day was spent till past 12 in a report made from the committee of privileges of the case between Sir William Egerton and Sir John Borlase, pretender to the election of Wiccomb. The committee had reported for Sir John Borlase, and the House agreed unto it.

Memo in this case: I were to have had it a void election and so were many of the House, but the major part were that Borlase's election was good:

1. It was a question whether the mayor was duly elected,

10. Grey does not report the Wiccomb election.

and consequently whether the return was good in point of form; but if the mayor be not the proper officer the return is not good.

2. It was doubtful whether the electors were duly qualified, they having been made very lately and on both sides merely to serve the turn of the several pretenders.

3. It was a question whether they went fairly to the poll, for Monday was appointed for it at a solemn meeting, and then it was anticipated, and made on the Friday before.

4. And lastly it was a very great question whether the poll were well taken or not, it being acknowledged by all to be taken at one time at two places by several persons at the two ends of a great hall; and the tellers who were for Sir William Egerton said Sir John Borlase had but 23 of the old burgesses, and the tellers for Sir John Borlase said he had 45 of the said old burgesses.

This was the substance of what I said: that for these reasons I thought the doubts too many for us to solve by a sudden vote, and the clearest way was to proceed to a new and fair election, which I humbly moved them to. This was seconded by my LORD ST. JOHN, BIRCH, SIR CHARLES HARBORD, and others, but [it] carried clearly for Sir John Borlase without dividing upon the question.

After this was done, SIR THOMAS MERES tendered a short bill for a test upon parliament men to be chosen for the future, but because it was late the Speaker would not receive it to be read; it being against the order of the House that any new bill should be read after twelve.

Then it was moved Sir Thomas Meres might report another case from the committee of elections; viz., that of Backwell and Mr. Wharton at Wendover, but it was said it would be long, and so put off till tomorrow.

Then MR. POWLE reported a clause to be added to the bill of indulgence concerning the renunciation of the covenant referred by order to a committee which was read, and passed, and the bill ordered to be engrossed.

COLONEL BIRCH spoke to the throwing out the clause as doing no good.

MR. VAUGHAN [spoke] against it as invading the act of indemnity for reasons so weak, or at least so obscure, as nobody was satisfied with, but the clause passed.

SIR JOHN DUNCOMBE spoke to casting out one half of the bill, taking only that part which was really indulgence, and leaving out that part which was for toleration.

SIR PHILLIP WARWICK spoke to leave out the words "of giving liberty to meet," and would put [in] words "that they should be free from punishment and penalties of former laws if they did meet"; but that was not thought important enough to alter the bill.

SIR JOHN BRAMSTON tendered a proviso that no man should have benefit by that bill but they who did first enter their names with the parson of the parish where they did live, and the name of the preacher whose congregation they would be of, but this would not be so much as read, so the bill was ordered to be engrossed.

Then it was moved by SIR JOHN COVENTRY that tomorrow be set apart to consider our grievances; and when it was said by some that it was unusual to make such general orders, there not appearing any ground for it, and that it was not parliamentary to do so, but where some grievances were named in which case it was usual to appoint a time to consider them; and this being insisted upon by MR. SOLICITOR, it was answered that they were ready to name them and

1. SIR THOMAS LEE mentioned an order of council by which 12d. per caldron was levied upon coal.

2. MR. POWLE complained of a proclamation by which the soldiers were exempted from civil justice.

3. SIR JOHN COVENTRY complained of half a crown per horse taken at Dover of all horses transported above the book of rates, which was proved by my LORD CASTLETON and SIR THOMAS CLERGES.

4. SIR TREVOR WILLIAMS complained of some proceedings

in Ireland, which would hazard that kingdom and put England to the expense of as much blood and treasure as it had formerly done.

5. SIR ROBERT HOLT complained of the levying of 2s. per annum of every smith's forge, which had been five times resolved against in that House.

6. SIR RICHARD EVERARD complained of the levying half a crown per annum of all licensed alehouses, on their recognizances, but this by color of the late paper act.

And so the order was made to proceed tomorrow at ten of the clock upon such grievances as now had been or should tomorrow be rendered to the House.

Tuesday March 18[11]

THE House passed the bill for taking of the aliens' customs for goods exported.

Then they proceeded on the grievances, and

1. SIR TREVOR WILLIAMS proceeded on the growth and increase of papists in Ireland and many particulars urged:

1. The King's order [of] February 1671 for admitting all papists in general into corporations.

2. The King's order for restraining Protestants from suing of papists for things done before the King's coming in.

3. The lessening the army there, and bringing many of them over hither, and disbanding some.

4. The exercising of episcopal jurisdiction by persons of the popish religion, especially by Peter Talbot.

5. The sending forth commissions to inquire into the estates of the Protestants there, to the great discouragement of all of that religion.

6. The employing of Colonel Richard Talbot as captain of a troop of horse there.

2. Then was urged the proclamation against coals.

11. Omitted in Grey.

3. Then the proclamation for exempting the soldiers from civil justice. So they called it, but in truth no such thing, nor any words of prohibition or restraint in the thing at all.

4. Then the quartering of soldiers [was] complained of by the LORD ST. JOHN and SIR JOHN NORTON, knights of the shire for Hampshire; the innkeepers being forced to give them their lodging, candles, and small beer for nothing, and besides that to advance them 5*d.* per diem in money; and some of these having 20, some 30 soldiers upon them.

SIR JOHN NORTON added that it was so in some private houses also.

All these the House voted should be humbly presented to his Majesty in an address. The smiths' forges, the injunction for the bankers, and the half crown upon recognizances for alehouse keepers were not mentioned.

5. They went upon the half crown taken at Dover for horses transported, and ordered James Housman who collected that duty to be sent for up.

In the afternoon the committee to whom these grievances were referred did meet; and Mr. Powle being in the chair did agree:

1. That his Majesty should be humbly supplicated to preserve the acts of settlement and explanation in Ireland inviolable.

2. That he would be pleased to recall his letters of February 1671, and the act of the council and proclamation issued thereupon in Ireland for the general admittance of papists into corporations in Ireland.

3. That no papists might be admitted into the army there, either as officer or soldier.

4. That no papist might be admitted to be either judge, justice of peace, sheriff, or coroner, or to be mayor, sovereign, or portreeve of any corporation.

5. That all archbishops, bishops, vicars general, and others

exercising ecclesiastical jurisdiction under the authority of the See of Rome may be by proclamation commanded to depart that kingdom, and if they do not, be prosecuted by law; and especially Peter Talbot, titular Archbishop of Dublin, for his notorious disloyalty to his Majesty, and contempt of his laws.

6. That all convents, seminaries, and public schools of papists may be dissolved, and all priests of regular orders commanded to depart the kingdom.

7. That Colonel Richard Talbot may be dismissed from his employment as captain of a troop of horse there, and may be forbidden to come within five miles of the court.

This last particular was voted *in terminis* by the House. The other grievances concerning England the committee did not go upon this night, but adjourned till tomorrow.

Wednesday March 19[12]

THE whole day spent upon the bill for indulgence which was brought in engrossed, and with some amendments passed, and ordered to be sent up to the Lords.

In the afternoon we went upon the bill for the highways, where I were in the chair.

Memo: I were not in the House at the putting of the question for passing the bill of indulgence, being sent out just before by Sir Edmund Godfrey, nor indeed did I much care to be, for I did not like the bill as thinking it a very great blow to the Church of England, and not easy to be recovered; and yet we had gone so far, both in the observation of the world, and in our engagement to the King by our address that something seemed necessary to be done in this matter, though I do not like the manner we have done it in; and I know many others are of my mind in the House, yet it passed with little opposition, and as little approbation.

12. Grey's account is fuller than Dering's.

Thursday March 20[13]

THIS day was spent in several small motions, and some particular bills read.

MR. SECRETARY COVENTRY informed us that his Majesty intended we should have a recess on this day seven night and therefore moved we should dispatch as well the bill for supply as any other public bills that were before us.

The bill for coinage passed to continue for seven years longer.

A bill for some jurisdiction to be placed in the dean and burgesses of Westminster.

A bill for freeing the citizens of London who are gone since the fire to inhabit in other parts from the duty of prizage and butlerage of wines, which those who continue living in London are free from was presented by MR. GARRAWAY, and read the first time, and cast out.

Friday [March] 21[14]

THIS day some private bills were read, and then the bill against popery was brought down from the Lords.

We called for the bill for the King's supply, which was ordered to be brought in engrossed this day, and was so. And many desired to proceed upon it, but it was moved that it might still lie upon the table till Tuesday, that so we might proceed upon the bill of popery now come down from the Lords. At last it was ordered to proceed on the bill against popery now, and to read the bill for the King's supply on Monday.

Then we proceeded on the amendments to the bill against popery, and the first that gave occasion of debate was the excusing of the Queen's servants from the oaths enjoined by

13. Grey's report is similar to Dering's.
14. Grey's account is much fuller than Dering's.

that bill, which was much spoken against by MR. POWLE, SIR THOMAS LEE, MR. WHORWOOD, and others.

THE ATTORNEY GENERAL, my LORD CORNBURY, SIR WILLIAM KILLEGREW, and MR. ATTORNEY MONTAGU spoke for it.

I ventured to propose a moderation in it, and that it might be allowed to the Queen's servants who were her servants in ordinary the first day of this session; that this could be of no ill consequence, the persons being few in number, and all known of peaceable behavior and none of them having ever appeared to be busy in matter of religion, or in perverting others; that by this means most of the inconveniences objected as possible would be prevented, for neither more nor worse disposed persons could come in, and we should show a respect to the King's power, which was not a little interested to preserve the articles of marriage; we should show a respect to the Queen who had deserved exceeding well from the whole nation, and we should not be in danger of any ill consequence by it. And if it were an exception of our act, it would do as exceptions are commonly held to do, rather to strengthen the rule than weaken it.[15]

The House seemed well inclined to this expedient, and the difficulty seemed chiefly to* be to find the means to do it, for where the Lords send us amendments we may reject part of that amendment, and agree to the rest of that amendment with what amendments we please of our own, but where they offered no words of theirs, but only left out some of our words, it was not so ready what to do, for here was nothing of the Lords to graft upon, and we could not amend our own bill.

But before this could be settled my LORD OF ANCRAM, speaking for compliance with the Lords, used this argument, that if we did subject the Queen's family to the law, hereafter no foreign princess of the popish religion would ever

* In the MS. a line is drawn down the margin from *to be to find* to the end of the entry for the day.

15. Grey does not report this speech.

match with our kings; which argument presently fixed the House against the proviso, for BIRCH replied that he was before of opinion for agreeing with the Lords, but now he retracted it, for if by subjecting the Queen's family to this law, we might forever keep our king from marrying of papists, it was the greatest reason in the world why we should stand upon it, for indeed he observed that this kingdom had never been in peace nor unity since the King's match with a woman of different religion; and presently the House voted not to agree with the amendment of the Lords.

Saturday March 22[16]

THE bill for uniting parishes in Exeter, reducing 17 churches to 8, was read the second time and committed.

Then we proceeded upon the bill of popery, and passed some particulars, and agreed and disagreed to others; but some being very long and intricate we referred them to a committee of the whole House, which did sit immediately.

And Sir Thomas Meres took the chair, but not going through them all they asked leave to sit again this afternoon; which was granted.

Post meridiem. The House ordered the committee of elections to try only the cases of Hythe and of Dartmouth, and the returns, not the merits of Thirsk and Malton, and to put off all other cases till after the recess.

Then we proceeded upon the rest of amendments to the bill of popery, and went through them. Then my Lord Cavendish stood up and said that it was now time to consider of our grievances; that some had been mentioned in the House, but not all; that it was fit now to give satisfaction to the people by considering who were the King's evil counsellors; that it

16. Grey's account is much fuller than Dering's.

was for the safety of the King and satisfaction of the people to inquire into them.

This was seconded by Mr. Sacheverell who said that we had gone very far in supplying the King, and had publicly by our bill owned the fears we had from the growth of popery; that it was inconsistent now to put all this money into the hands of a favorer of the popish party; and that we ought to make a humble address to his Majesty to remove that great officer from that trust; that he knew nothing himself by him, but had it from common fame, and desired not the ruin of the man but the safety of the kingdom.

Mr. Mallet thirded this matter, adding that my Lord Treasurer (whom the two others had not named) was a known enemy of the Protestant religion, and had, in the House of Lords, said that this bill against popery was a dirty bill, and destined to be spurned out of the House.

Colonel Sandys spoke against prosecuting any man upon public fame; instanced in my Lord of Strafford, where innocent blood, and so confessed afterwards, was shed upon that account.

Sir John Birkenhead [said] that we should, in this bill before us, put such tests upon all officers as would discover who were papists or not.

Sir William Doyley [said] that it was a mistake to think this money or any part of it could be disposed by the treasurer alone, many other officers must concur and the King himself must sign it.[17]

Monday October 20[1]

THIS day the House did meet according to the adjournment made before the recess; viz., 29 March last, but it being known that the King had resolved for some reasons to determine this

17. Dering does not report the debates for March 24, 25, 27, 28, and 29, but he was named for committees on March 24, 25, and 27. (*C.J.*, IX, 274, 275, 278.)

1. Omitted in Grey.

session by a short prorogation, it was generally conceived that nothing at all would be spoken or moved, and it was ordered (as it was said) that to prevent any occasion of discourse Mr. Speaker should not take the chair till the Black Rod were ready to come to the door. Accordingly he came not till half an hour past ten. As soon as he was come, and sat down by the table, the House with some earnestness called "to the chair, to the chair"; which he not taking notice of, it was said if he would not take the chair, some other should. Then he said it was the constant custom to go to prayers first, and after that, he would take the chair.

SIR ROBERT THOMAS said that prayers was but a ceremony, and might be dispensed with.

Then MR. POWLE said if he would not take the chair, he would speak to him where he was; whereupon he was forced to take the chair, for those that did not desire it could not well speak against his taking the chair, being present and a full House.

As soon as he was seated, MR. POWLE said he knew his time was but short, and therefore his speech should not be long, but what he had to say was of concern to the whole nation; that we had been very careful to prevent popery, but it was in vain to suppress it elsewhere if it got footing so near the throne; that the Duke of York had intentions to marry a papist, an Italian lady of the House of Modena, kin to two cardinals; and his humble motion was that we might make an address to the King that this intended match may not be consummated. This was seconded by COLONEL BIRCH, who said that from the first intention of the Spanish match to this day, all our troubles had had their rise from these popish alliances.

SIR THOMAS CLERGES added that the King of France but two years since, when his brother, the Duke of Orleans, had married a Protestant lady, daughter of the Palatinate, although one of the articles were that she should enjoy her religion, yet as soon as she came to Metz was by a messenger from the King of France obliged either to change her religion or to forbear coming into France.

Little was opposed to this, but THE SECRETARY and SIR JOHN DUNCOMBE spoke something to it; as that it was but by common fame we knew there was such a match, which was not sufficient for us to ground a bill upon and an address to the King; and again, that for ought they knew the match was already consummated, and so this address moved came too late, or something to this purpose.

But the motion for the address being followed by SIR ROBERT HOWARD with expressions that the danger of popery was now greater than ever, it was put to the question and passed with little contradiction.

By this time the Black Rod was at the door, and the House, being called up to the Lords' House, was then prorogued for seven days.

Monday October 27[2]

THIS day we met again, and being called up to the Lords, the King, and after him, the lord chancellor opened the cause of the meeting, which at his return the Speaker acquainted us with, reading the King's speech, which was, in short, to tell us he had hoped to have welcomed us with an honorable peace, but was hindered from it by that insolence of the Dutch who would not admit of any terms that were equal, and had treated his ambassador at Cologne with contempt; and therefore he desired a supply, and that it might be speedy and proportioned to his occasions. In the next place, he promised to comply with them in what they should desire for the security of religion and property, which he had always been tender of. In the 3rd place, he recommended the case of the bankers to our consideration.

2. Grey's account is not so full as Dering's.

As to my Lord Chamberlain's speech, MR. SPEAKER told us he spoke so low he could not well hear him.

Upon this was moved, (I think by MR. STOCKDALE) that the consideration of this speech might be put off till Friday, which was seconded by others.

It was not opposed at all, but it was moved by THE SECRE- TARY, and seconded by SIR JOHN DUNCOMBE, and thirded by THE ATTORNEY GENERAL that we might give his Majesty thanks for that part of his speech which concerned our reli- gion and property, as we had done before upon the like occa- sion, and had been practice in Queen Elizabeth's time.

This was opposed by MR. SACHEVERELL, SIR JOHN HOT- HAM, MR. GARRAWAY, and others, saying that it would be time enough on Friday when we had considered the whole speech.

And so it was laid by.

After this was over, SIR THOMAS LITTLETON in a set speech moved that we might have another Speaker because he was a privy councillor and so not proper to be trusted with the secrets of the House; secondly, because being in that high sphere he was now above the place of Speaker, nor was it fit he, who was now one of the governors of the world, should be servant to the House of Commons; 3rdly, that he had other eminent places and employment which would take up his time so much as he could not attend the services of the House with that diligence he ought to do; and lastly, that the House had formerly occasion to question the management of the treasury of the navy, and if it should have to again it would be a very unkind thing that he who is questioned should sit in the chair at the debates, when it was not fit he should so much as hear the debates. And therefore prayed him to leave the chair, and that they might chose another Speaker *pro tempore* to debate this matter.

This was opposed by SIR JOSEPH TREDINHAM, COLONEL STRANGWAYS, SIR JOHN BIRKENHEAD, SIR COURTENAY

POOLE, MR. SOLICITOR, and others because there are several precedents of privy councillors that have been Speakers: Sir Thomas Hungerford, Mr. Heigham, and Sir William Cordell[3] (to which I think may be added Sir John Baker, 1 Ed. 6th) but no footstep of any one that ever was removed or so much as questioned for being a privy councillor. That the reasons had no weight at all; that he took no other oath to the King than other privy councillors did, and by the same reason we might move all privy councillors out of the House. That for his employments if he did neglect the service of the House, which none could say he yet had done, it would be then reasonable to take notice of.

The truth is there was not so much said for the Speaker as might have been, but there was not much need of it, for all precedents were full for him and none at all against him.

Then MR. WILLIAM HERBERT made a long speech against him; that he was not fit to be Speaker because the honor of the House did suffer by his being a common gamester and that in public places, but this made no impression with the House.

And then MR. HOWE stood up and said he had other matter of greater weight to lay to his charge, and that was he had used opprobrious words of the whole House, having called them a company of curs, and that Mr. Hopkins, and Sir Thomas Meres, and my Lord St. John had heard them.

MR. HOPKINS said indeed he had heard the words, but he took them but as raillery, to which he himself had given the occasion; for telling the Speaker that he was very nimble, and had started from his seat as quick as a hare from her form, the Speaker replied he had reason to do so, when such curs were at his heels.

But this was not thought ingenious to pursue a man for an ill-weighed word, and which indeed considering the preced-

3. Sir Thomas Hungerford was Speaker in 1414, Sir Clement Heigham in 1554, and Sir William Cordell in 1558.

ent discourse which induced it, it was no more than continuing that Mr. Hopkins had begun, without any malice in the thing at all.

Mr. Garraway* said that it was not reasonable to call any gentleman to account for words so long time after; that by order of parliament if any man took offense he was to do it before the House rose, that the matter being fresh no mistake might be run into, and that none were to be questioned the next day, and much less in another session as this was now.

Colonel Birch made a material difference upon this point, and that was when words were spoken in parliament upon any debate then the exception was to be taken presently, but words spoken out of parliament as these were might be questioned at any time, and if they were against the honor of the House when was the time to question them but when the parliament did meet next.

Upon the whole matter the debate grew flat and cold, and most were willing to let it go off without a question, but Sir Thomas Littleton and Mr. Howe insisting to have the question put, which having been firsted and seconded could not be denied, the previous question being put (the main question being whether the Speaker should leave the chair and the House choose a new Speaker *pro tempore*) it was carried in the negative, there being 300 in the House, not above twenty affirmatives.

Then we proceeded to appoint days according to custom for the grand committees of grievances, trade, and courts of justice, but religion was forgotten and elections put off till Thursday.

Then we read a bill which is customary at the first beginning of a session; and it was a bill for repairing of churches by laying a rate upon the inhabitants.

Memo: I question whether it were regular to bring in this

* In the MS. a line is drawn down the margin for the next two paragraphs.

bill without order of the House, it being for raising money upon the subject by a tax. But the desire the House had to read a bill, which was a kind of settling the Speaker in his place, outweighed that consideration, there being no other bill ready.

They made also a committee to inspect the entries made in the journal the last session, which is not usual to make a private committee before the grand committee and committee of elections.

And so we adjourned till Thursday next.

Besides this it was moved by SIR JOHN MOUNSON that the House might keep solemnly the 5th of December[4] and that Dr. Stillingfleet be entreated to preach before us at St. Margaret's; which was ordered.

Thursday October 30[5]

THIS day MR. SECRETARY COVENTRY tendered to us the King's answer to our address concerning the Duke's marriage, having first desired to know the pleasure of the House, because the order was made for the address in the last session. The answer was in writing: that he had proceeded so far in that match as he could not now comply with the desires of the parliament, and that he did not believe that it had been ungrateful to them because a former match with a princess of the same religion had been long in agitation, and the parliament had taken no notice at all of it or expressed any dissatisfaction in it.

After a long silence in the House MR. STOCKDALE began to move the House that, notwithstanding this letter, we should proceed to make a new address to the King to prevent the consummation of this marriage. This was seconded by BIRCH,

4. Really November.
5. Grey gives a full report, but the order of debate differs from that reported by Dering.

SIR THOMAS CLERGES, SIR THOMAS MERES, MR. POWLE and others; opposed by SECRETARY COVENTRY, MR. WALLER, LORD ANCRAM, SIR THOMAS HIGGONS, SIR ROBERT CARR, and MR. ATTORNEY.

The arguments were chiefly from the King's honor deeply engaged; the marriage already completed; the unreasonableness of asking what is not in the King's power to do if he should be willing; the danger of having a litigious and disputable issue if the Duke should now marry another. At last being put to question, there were 186 for the address, and but 88 against it.[6] Then they named a committee to draw up the address.

Then MR. CHEYNEY moved that the House might be called over, and that every man might give satisfaction to the House if he had taken the tests enjoined by the late act.

But MR. GARRAWAY said he desired to carry it a little further; and that a bill be brought in to make all those who should not take such tests as should thereby be thought fit to be imposed for the discovery of popery, incapable of any employment civil or military, and of sitting in either house of parliament, and of coming within five miles of the court; which was ordered accordingly.

This day we proceeded also upon judging the return of Thirsk; and calling for the clerk of the crown with the returns, it appearing that Sir William Wentworth was returned by the proper officer, and so acknowledged by the other party, but only alleging that the officer was a papist, which did not appear; and if it were so, yet being actually in the place and none there but he, it was to be presumed he was so that was acknowledged so by both parties. The House determined the merits of the returns, leaving the merit of the election to the committee for elections.

In the midst of this debate MR. SACHEVERELL moved that he saw a gentleman in the House whom he conceived to be no member, and therefore all debates should cease while he

6. In the *Journal* (IX, 284) the affirmatives are recorded as 184.

was in the House. The gentleman he meant was Sir Paul Neale. It was presently moved he should withdraw; others said he was returned by the clerk of the crown, and had taken the oaths, and therefore was to sit; but it was said that was well where the House wanted a member, but they conceived the House was full before (for he came in for Newark which had a patent for choosing burgesses newly granted from the King). It was said that however he ought to be heard in his place what he could say for himself; and as he was going to speak it was said by others that if he would speak at all he must speak at the Bar; that to speak in his place was only the privilege of a member. At last he thought it advisable to withdraw without speaking at all, and the House ordered his case to be taken into consideration on Tuesday next.

Then the House named the committee of elections, there being hardly any precedent that we had sat two days, and named two other committees, and not yet named that committee.

They added to this committee that all that come should have voices.

Friday October 31[7]

THE House this morning took into consideration the King's speech, which, being chiefly for money for supply of the war, and for payment of the bankers, Mr. Russell first began, and declared his judgment that we should pass a negative vote that we should give no money. This was seconded by Sir John Hotham, by Lord Cavendish, and very eloquently in a set speech by Sir John Mounson; but after an hour's discourse, this being shown to be too harsh and incongruous by Mr. Secretary Coventry, Sir Robert Howard, and others, then Mr. Sacheverell delivered in a question in writing that we should give no money till the ten months which are already charged

7. Grey's report is fuller than Dering's.

by the last bill for supply were elapsed, not till our grievances were effectively redressed.

This took up the whole day, all consenting that grievances should be redressed, but many opposing the restraint of time, from the inconveniences which might arise though not now foreseen. Many digressions were made upon the grievances we lie under, and which were fit to be redressed: the war with Holland, the league with France, the dangers from popish counsels and counsellors, the standing army, and many others. These were instanced and dilated on by Sir Thomas Lee, Mr. Garraway, Lord Cornbury, Sir William Coventry, and others. Mr. Powle added also the preferring of my Lord Lauderdale to the government of Scotland, and my Lord Anglesey to the privy seal. Sir Thomas Clerges mentioned the giving away 400,000*l*. in gratuities since May last; and Mr. Howe and Mr. Powle both made it one of their grievances that the Speaker being a privy councillor did keep that chair. This held, banding to and fro, till after 4 of the clock Sir William Coventry proposed that those negative words might stand, with this addition, "unless the obstinacy of the Dutch shall render it necessary." These words were said with great consent of the House, and so it passed.

Then the House read over an address in writing to be presented to the King by the Speaker, containing reasons why we did desire his Majesty to hinder the consummation of the marriage of his Royal Highness with the Princess of Modena.

Saturday November 1[1]

THE House met this day in the afternoon in expectation that the King would have given them leave to attend him at this time with the address concerning the Princess of Modena, but his Majesty appointed Monday in the afternoon, so the House only revived the committee for the bill for tests against popery, and adjourned.

1. Omitted in Grey.

Monday November 3[2]

THE House began with a consideration of an address to be made to the King for a public fast, which was presented from the committee by SIR THOMAS CLERGES, and approved by the House, [and] was ordered to be sent up to the Lords for their concurrence.

Then the House being very still, and nothing moved, I moved them to give a second reading to the bill for repairs of parish churches, and providing for recovery of small tithes, which was read accordingly.

It was objected against it by MR. BOSCAWEN and MR. MORRIS that it was imperfect because there was not sufficient provisions for taking the accounts, and that more power ought to be left in the justices of peace which was reasonable, for I that moved for it, did not think it a good bill as it is, but because the end was acknowledged by all to be good, it was worthy our pains to amend it; so it was committed.

Then MR. THOMAS MORRIS tendered a bill for preventing of stealing away children, and making it felony without clergy; but because it was thought there was an office in the belly, it being provided that all that go over to the plantations as servants shall enter their names somewhere, the House, which is always averse to any project of that nature, would not receive it, or go on upon it, though it had been once read, but ordered him to withdraw it, and ordered a committee to bring in another for that purpose.

Then COLONEL BIRCH moved for a bill for naturalization of foreigners, and used the common arguments for it.

After him SIR THOMAS MERES stood up, and said he was for the thing moved, but not for the way. He said he desired to increase our people not so much by bringing in foreigners, as by taking away all those occasions that made these we have of our own useless and unprofitable by bringing them up in lewd and disorderly courses, of which the first and greatest

2. Grey's report is confined to the debate on a standing army.

was the continuance of a standing army; that it was the chief
of our grievances, and the cause of many other, and therefore in the first place and before all other he desired we
would vote it to be a grievance. This was seconded by COLO-
NEL BIRCH, SIR THOMAS LEE, SIR HENRY CAPELL, etc. MR.
SECRETARY COVENTRY [said] that this, properly speaking,
was neither a standing army nor a grievance; not a standing
army because it was now raised upon a visible necessity, being
in a war with the Dutch, who might land elsewhere they
please; nor was it a grievance properly because a grievance
is supposed always to be against law, and no man did deny
but the raising of soldiers was in the King's power when he
thought fit; and that some of them were already ordered to
go to Ireland, and the rest would be disbanded as soon as the
kingdom was in peace.

MR. POWLE urged that it was in the power of the King to
raise funds in time of rebellion at home, or in case of a foreign war, but not then to keep them here, but to transport
them where the seat of the war was; that it was plain in this
case, that this army was not raised to maintain the war, but
the war was made to have an occasion and pretense to raise
this army; that we did all see what service they had done,
which was no more than to make a formidable march from
Blackheath to Yarmouth; that the pretense of landing in
Zealand was so improbable and indeed impossible, that it
could not sink into any man's imagination that it was ever
really intended; that what good could be intended to the
nation, from that army which was commanded by a foreigner
(Count Schomburg), and had for his major-general an Irish
papist (viz., Colonel Fitzgerald).

Upon the whole, the question being put whether a standing
army be a grievance, it passed with full consent, there being
but three negatives. After the question [was] put and voted
and declared for the affirmative, MR. SACHEVERELL, instead
of the word "a standing army," repeated it with the word

"the," and so I believe it is entered, though it was easy to observe some difference in those words.

Then SIR THOMAS MERES moved that a committee might be made to draw up an address to the King upon this grievance. MR. CHEYNEY moved that might be let alone till all the grievances were gone through, and then by one address to represent the whole, which was more parliamentary, would save our time, and would go with more weight. But this was opposed by MR. SACHEVERELL, and so a committee was ordered to draw up an address for this particular.[3]

3. On November 4 the parliament was prorogued to January 7, 1673–4.

Index